DinnerOnTime

Holiday & Special Occasion Cooking Preparation Guidelines & Shopping Lists

Janne Taubman

First printing 2001

ISBN 0-9705739-0-1

Cooking and preparations times may differ from those in the plans based on the kitchen appliances used, knowledge base, and cooking skill of the purchaser. Individuals should read the entire menu and preparation time table before beginning any preparation.

Printed and bound in the United States of America

Design and layout by Lead Dog Communications; 970/482-0318; www.LeadDogCommunications.com

Table of Contents

Dedicated to my mother, Rita Beuchat Sexton, who showed me the way

Acknowledgments

Thanks to Chrissy De Jack, Nancy Lang, Barb Wilson, Elizabeth Gaydos, Pat Simmons, Tammy Rogers, Linda Carlson, Jolene Crowley, Pam Heyer, Jill Gotschalk, Gotschalk's Graphics, Milinda J. Crispin, Sue Tabadisto, Chris Gosset, Kristin Brennan, Diana Bors, Kathy Aldrich, Paula Van Dyne, and Nancy Greystone who contributed by critiquing my food, menus and timetables, and in general, supported this endeavor.

Thanks also to my husband, Scott, and my daughter and husband, Kristen and Adam Lee, and many friends and family who encouraged me and believed in Dinner On Time.

Introduction

I come from a family of eight children. In retrospect, it seems to me that a great deal of our waking hours were spent around food—planning what to eat, preparing it, and doing the dishes for ten people. Cooking for that crowd made every dinner a major production and as each of us grew older, we were enlisted to help in the preparations. It seemed that I intuitively learned how to prepare large quantities of food and to time the preparations in such a way so as to get everything on the table at the same time.

Now that I have my own family and home, I find that one of my favorite things to do is cook. I love to try new recipes and be innovative in recipe interpretation and entertaining. Friends always seem to enjoy coming to our home for dinner and frequently comment on how easy I make it look. But, when I say that it really *is* easy, numerous guest decry that it is not so for them. Many a time, I have tried to share menus and recipes but it seems knowing what to cook isn't the challenge. It's the planning and scheduling.

Recently, a friend was asking me for basic recipes for a Thanksgiving dinner. For the very first time, she was preparing the traditional sit-down dinner for a large group, seventeen in all. I could see that it truly was overwhelming her and so I offered to go to her home, recipes in hand, and help her plan the dinner. We created the menu, wrote out the recipes with detailed directions, made a shopping list, wrote out an hourly plan for preparation based on when she wanted to sit down to eat, and even put Post-it notes in serving dishes so she would know what went where. The process took us about three hours. And her dinner turned out exactly as she hoped it would.

When I was relating this story to a friend, she suggested I write a book. She believed there are many people, especially new cooks, who have a difficult time entertaining and making sure everything ends up on the table at the same time. A little research showed that while there are numerous cookbooks and guides to entertaining, there wasn't any cookbook to walk someone through the process from planning to "show time." I thought it would be fun to take a crack at it and here is my best effort!

When individuals have shared their recipes with me, I have tried to give credit where credit is due. Some recipes have come from cookbooks, the majority of which I have altered over the years to suit our tastes. By giving you examples, I hope to show you a process that is transferable to any other culinary event you wish to plan. Enjoy!

Janne Taubman

Planning

A Year-Long Process

Most of us are busy people who rush from one day's events to another. Special occasions that require a great deal of time and preparation seem to sneak up on us. We know that they are coming, but we're not quite sure how they got here already. So when they jump out at us, we generally feel that we have no time to really plan ahead, and at the last minute, are doing our best to pull it together. We always promise ourselves that the *next time* we will be better prepared and plan ahead.

How many times have you gone to the store to purchase something that is essential to your project, only to realize that you had seen it on sale previously? You shrug your shoulders and vow that *next time* you're going to plan ahead and buy it when you see it advertised as a "special." This happened to me one year when I saw the candlestick holders that I had purchased right before Christmas, marked down to half price in the January sales! I promised myself that I was never going to let that happen again, even if it meant waiting a year to sport that kind of accessory.

This kind of self-discipline doesn't happen over night; it takes some planning and forethought too. Begin to notice patterns that have developed around your entertaining...the kinds of meals you like to serve, the recipes that you find yourself repeating with some frequency, and the decorations you like to display on your tables. Do you always have pumpkin or cherry pie on Thanksgiving or use red candles at Christmas? With some conscious thought, you can begin to watch for items as you move through the year and get them when they are at their lowest price.

Where food is concerned, pay attention to those recipes that are your good old "stand-bys." Watch for coupons and sales of the required nonperishable ingredients and purchase them ahead of time. Not only does it allow you to get them at the best price but it also helps to spread the cost of major events such as Passover and Thanksgiving over the year instead of it hitting all at once. Know that you'll be hosting the family reunion in August? It takes discipline, but think about the menu in March so you can watch for items, including paper goods, as they show up in "off-season" sales. And you will always have some things on hand for "drop ins." I always have the ingredients for Ethyl's Cream Cheese Spread and Kristen's Pasta in my pantry!

China, Crystal, and Decorations

Most of us don't sit down to dinner every night with our family at a table that is set with a beautiful centerpiece, candles, and our best silver and china. What a pity! But if you think that entertaining is something that you really want to get into, then there are some basics in which you probably want to invest. Most of us are not fortunate enough to purchase all of the accoutrements at once, but thoughtful planning can ensure that as you do begin to collect the tools and decorations that add convenience and fun to your entertaining, they will all be compatible.

I have learned that even the most basic of dinners, like meatloaf, can be special when beautifully presented on an elegant, candle-lit table. Everyday tableware can be "dressed up" fairly easily and there are many occasions that don't necessarily lend them selves to china. In other words, you don't have to spend big bucks on china and crystal before you can have a lovely dinner party or a Christmas buffet for you friends. You can create your own elegance with a few inexpensive investments. Add to your collection as the years, and sales roll by, knowing that additions match what you already have in your cupboards.

If you are setting up housekeeping for the first time, it's important to spend sometime thinking about what really appeals to you in the way of everyday tableware, china, crystal and flatware. If you already have dishes, china, and crystal but want to expand or change your theme, you may still be well served by following a process. Visit department stores, outlet centers, and stores such as Cost Plus and Pier One and explore your options, taking into consideration what you can afford at the time.

If your taste isn't inclined toward china and crystal or if they are going to have to be on your wish list, consider an everyday set of dishes for at least eight, that is very plain and simple and lends itself to being "dressed up" for company. Chunky, earthenware dishes with a southwestern influence may seem sensible for every day use but won't lend themselves to doubling for china as well as a plain white plate. If white seems a little too boring, any plain solid color that blends with a variety of other colors will be more flexible. China-looking plates with a subdued print can work well also.

If your goal is to have service for more than eight, call the china company and make sure the pattern you choose is not going to be discontinued soon. Plan to purchase additional sets as your budget allows until you can serve your desired number of guest.

Or consider doing what my husband and I did. When we were married, we selected a moderately priced china and crystal pattern, and hoped that family and friends would begin to build our collection. Early on, we knew that we would be having large numbers of people, sometimes up to thirty, for holiday parties and Passover, but there was no way that we could afford to buy china and crystal all once for that crowd! Instead, we went shopping at Pier One and over the period of about six months purchased from their stock dishes thirty white dinner, salad, and dessert plates; the same number of soup bowls; twenty cups and saucers, and several platters and serving dishes. We talked with the manager and learned that they planned to carry this line of dishes for at least the next year. We decided to take the risk they were good on their word. We already had a number of silver serving dishes that would compliment the "china." We kept a serving for eight in our "everyday" cupboard and the rest went into the china cabinet.

Next, we bought twenty-four plain Libby wine glasses. Certainly not fine crystal, but with the lights low and an abundance of candlelight, we could get a semblance of a sparkle from them. We also didn't worry about having the correctly shaped wine glass for the appropriate wine. (As I recall, when we first started entertaining, we were into jug wine anyway.) We also bought standard tumblers for mixed drinks and tall glasses for water and milk in the same quantities. Most of our very large gatherings include some children, thus the reasoning behind only purchasing two dozen wine glasses and twenty cups and saucers. There was little chance that all of the glasses or cups would ever be used at the same time.

We also couldn't afford stainless steel silverware so we shopped the sales and bought inexpensive flatware. We chose the pattern that seemed to feel the heaviest while being very plain and simple. We still use that same flatware for our large sit down dinners and do not commingle it with the everyday stainless silverware that we finally purchased.

While you are window shopping, look at glasses, crystal and flatware so you can get a feel for what you like to see together. Also keep in mind that most sets of dishes only come with one platter and one serving dish, so you'll need to be on the lookout for extra serving dishes. Dishes that are white, or at least have a white background, lend themselves to an easier match if you wish to buy extra pieces off the shelf.

No matter when you choose to buy "good" china, crystal and flatware, you should go through the same window shopping drill you did for your everyday ware. If you are not going to purchase all three at the same time, I recommend you start with the china. You want to make sure that subsequent selections of crystal and silverware complement the very visible dishes on your table. Many fine patterns of well-known companies, such as Lennox, Noritake, and Gorham, are available for years. Consider choosing all three at the same time even if initially you are only going to be investing in the china. Remember that additions to your collection can make wonderful holiday or birthday presents from friends and family. It's fine to acquire your china one plate at a time, especially when they are on sale, and before you know it, you'll be having a dinner party for four with your new settings.

Linen, Accessories, and Centerpieces

This is where your personality and creativity can really shine. Again, start simple and build on what you have.

For a more causal setting with your "everyday" dishes, I recommend purchasing a set of plain place mats that compliment your dishes. If your plates are plain, you can cleverly change the mood and the degree of "dress up" simply by changing the napkins that complement a plain place mat and dish. A plain matching napkin is more elegant that a plaid one. You'll have two different settings by having added only one set of napkins. Shop the sales for napkin rings that will again change the whole feel of your setting. You can sometimes find them for as little as a dollar a piece. Purchase a yard or so of pretty ribbon and tie a bow around the napkin. Again, plain dishes and napkins allow you more flexibility when choosing ribbons or unique napkin rings.

To dress up the table even more, replace the mats with a tablecloth. Make sure you purchase linens that are washable and permanent press. Before setting the table, you can wet one of the napkins and throw them all in the dryer for a few minutes to remove the wrinkles; immediately put on the table and smooth.

If you've chosen your everyday ware and china thoughtfully, your tablecloth will work with both. You should eventually purchase a table pad to protect the surface of the table and that also lends a feel to the table that is more elegant. There are many different kinds on the market but I believe that the large sheet, one side heavy plastic and the other side flannel, is the best buy. It can easily be folded to accommodate a smaller table with extensions and is easy to store. The more expensive pads have to be ordered for your table.

Once you have one tablecloth, one set of place mats and two sets of napkins, you can add variety to your collection when the sales come around but planning ahead is a must. Buy next year's Christmas tablecloth during the January sales!

I believe candles can add to and change the atmosphere at any table. Today, there is such a variety from which to choose that you can creatively change the look of your table, even when you are using the same tablecloth, mats, and napkins all of the time. Again, start with one basic set of candlestick holders for a standard taper candle. Choose silver, brass, or crystal, depending on what you feel looks best with your table setting.

Once you have the basics, you can begin to have some real fun with candles. There are as many kinds, sizes, and shapes as there are colors. You can even mix and match on the same table. Consider using four or six small, clear votives with colored candles down the center of your casual table or use one at each place setting. Or choose tall glass holders that "float" standard taper candles in water; they are very festive and can add elegance to any special occasion. You're limited only by your imagination and money.

Candles can be expensive. You can buy the same basic candles at Payless, Tuesday Morning, K-Mart, or Wal-Mart for much less, sometimes even half the price, than you'll find in a candle shop or department store. You won't find many unique or specialty candles there. When you do find something unique, let it burn down an inch or so and place a small tea light in the middle and burn that wick instead. Eventually, the candle may begin to fade; if so, burn the candle. Watch for sales and buy in large quantities when available.

Centerpieces can also be fun and unique. A small crystal bowl filled with cut flowers and flanked with candles is always simple and lovely. Using flowers from your garden and yard will add a variety of flowers and greens as the seasons change. Plant some spring bulbs in a bowl and watch them bloom in front of your eyes. You can always buy cut flowers at the grocery store and make your own arrangements if you don't have a garden of your own.

I like to use candles as the centerpiece itself. Float several candles (made for that purpose) in your crystal bowl. Add fresh cranberries to the bowl along with the candles and you have a wonderful Christmas centerpiece. Or place several three-inch or wider candles on decorative holders that are different heights. The number and the sizes can be as many as the table will allow. This lends itself well to a casual or elegant table

Consider using different kinds of glass holders that use standard taper candles and mix with ones that use oil and a wick. Use a variety of sizes, shapes, and heights to create a very different kind of look each time you set the table. You don't need to use pairs of holders and can also vary the color of the candles and the oil as well. Create an elegant look by using white, gold, or silver candles with clear oil in the glass holders. Change it again by tying wide ribbon bows around the holders.

Last New Year's Eve, I purchased several different sizes and shapes of clear Christmas tree balls—the ones with the rainbow effect. I turned them upside down and placed them individually in candlestick holders that were of various heights and shapes and mingled them with other holders that held candles or oil. The centerpiece was very unusual and received many compliments. This is a good time to use a candlestick that has lost its partner due to breakage. Never throw anything away!

During the year, keep your eyes open for unusual pieces of crystal, napkin rings, place cards, pieces of ribbon, or other items that can be used to enhance or change the look of the same old tablecloth.

Index of Recipes

DINNER FOR SIXTEEN: THANKSGIVING

Jalapeño Jelly Over Cream Cheese
Tom Turkey Stuffed With Traditional Bread Stuffing
Mashed Potatoes and Gravy
Cranberry Sauce
Steamed Broccoli
Celery and Mushrooms
Thyme Corn
Rolls
Black Olives
Pumpkin Pie With Whipped Cream

Thanksgiving is one of my favorite holidays, but the meal preparation can be stressful. I usually make way too much of everything—but there can't be too many leftovers, can there? The biggest challenge, of course, is getting everything on the table at the same time with the hot things hot and the cold things cold.

I always start at least a week ahead of time by planning the menu and the grocery list. Our family has its traditions, which really don't vary from year to year. Occasionally, I'll try to slip in something new because I enjoy trying out recipes, but I haven't been very successful in changing the menu.

I have used smaller recipe sizes; simply double or triple as needed. Please read this plan in its entirety before beginning any preparations.

Planning: Because of the amount of food on the table, I like to keep the centerpiece small and simple. I usually place a few candles of varying heights in the center of the table to make it festive but leaving enough room for all the serving dishes. Choose your colors based on your dishes and tablecloth.

Whether you're feeding 4 or 24, the following menu stays the same. It will simply be the amounts and preparation time that change.

Jalapeño Jelly Over Cream Cheese

8-ounce jar jalapeño jelly
8-ounce package cream cheese
assorted crackers

Guests usually arrive about 2 hours before the meal—smelling that turkey roasting is half of the pleasure! If you plan on serving drinks before the meal, have a little something to nibble on but don't put out a spread that will fill them up and not leave room for the dinner. Do something simple that doesn't take any time. Buy a jar of jalapeño jelly (I make my own in the fall and it's the best, but we'll leave that for another holiday party!) and serve over a block of cream cheese with crackers.

Tip: To help simplify things, you can just put out a bowl of mixed nuts to serve as an appetizer.

Tom Turkey Stuffed With Traditional Bread Stuffing

20- to 22-pound turkey
Traditional Bread Stuffing
1 onion, outer skin peeled off and quartered
1 stalk celery, leaves included
1 carrot, quartered
1bay leaf
fresh ground pepper
margarine or butter for basting

This size turkey will generously feed up to 16 people with a few leftovers. Even if we only have 6 at our table, we *still* prepare this size bird because we love the leftovers. If entertaining more than 16, add another pound for each guest, and add a few more pounds if you want leftovers.

Many people like a fresh turkey the best. Some believe they are fresher and not stringy like some frozen turkeys can be. They are more expensive, however, and must be ordered from the butcher at least a week to 10 days ahead of time.
If you use a frozen turkey, purchase it the weekend before Thanksgiving so you can thaw it according to the instructions on the package. It should be defrosted in the refrigerator to protect against food poisoning. It must be completely defrosted the day before so you can get the giblets out of the bird to begin preparation. A 20- to 22-pound turkey will take five to six days to defrost in the refrigerator. You don't want to put a turkey in the oven that is even partially frozen, as it will be difficult to gage cooking time.

The day before, remove the neck and giblets (heart, gizzard, and liver) from the turkey and place them in a large saucepan. Add the onion, celery, carrot, bay leaf, and about four good "turns" of pepper from the mill. (Wash the vegetables before placing in the pan.) Cover all with water (about 6 to 8 cups). Bring to a boil, then simmer for about 45 minutes. Cool, cover, and put entire saucepan and contents in the refrigerator.

While your broth is simmering, wash the turkey inside and out with cold water. (Care should always be taken when preparing fowl so as to prevent salmonella or other food poisoning. Always wash hands before and after handling the bird. Don't stuff the bird until right before putting it into the oven; the warm dressing invites the growth of bacteria.) Check the skin for any pinfeathers that were not removed. Dry off and place in the refrigerator in a large plastic bag.

Traditional Bread Stuffing

There are as many recipes for dressing as there are families! I prefer my mom's recipe, all made from scratch. It takes more time, but it's worth it. If you must, you can use a boxed stuffing mix; follow the directions on the box.

1½ loaves white bread
3 cups chopped celery
3 cups chopped onion, preferably white
¾ cup margarine or butter
1½ to 3 cups turkey broth (see above instructions for giblet preparation)
4 tablespoons rubbed sage (dried leaf that is crushed but not ground)

Remove the bread from wrapper the day before and spread out on cookie sheets to dry. Turn occasionally. Later that day or night, tear into small pieces and place in a very large bowl. (Before I acquired a large bowl, I used a medium-sized trash bag. It sounds strange, but it works well and it will be out of the way before company arrives!) Make sure you keep the pieces small; large pieces can cause dressing to be less fluffy and denser. Leave bread out overnight to continue the drying process.

Chop the onion and celery the day before as well. Place in an airtight container or Ziploc bag and store in the refrigerator. (You can do this on Thanksgiving morning, but you'll have to start your preparations a half hour earlier.)

If you wish to make more or less dressing, follow this formula: For each half loaf of bread, use 1 cup each of onion and celery, all of the giblets,

1 1/3 tablespoon sage and ¼ cup butter. Use about ½ to 1 cup broth to bind the dressing together.

We usually eat at about 6 o'clock on Thanksgiving. This allows me to sleep in a little on the holiday and take my time with the preparations. When I was growing up, I remember Mama getting up some years at six o'clock in the morning to get the bird in the oven so we could eat in the early afternoon. Not me! Sitting down at six allows me to amble through the day and even take a little rest before the guests arrive.

Whatever your preference is for dinner time, you'll need to start the dressing preparation approximately 1 hour before you want to put the bird in the oven. When I begin to make the dressing, I take the turkey out of the refrigerator and allow it to come closer to room temperature. Again, stuff the turkey immediately before putting the bird in the oven, or you run the risk of food poisoning.

Melt butter or margarine in a very large skillet and add onion and celery. Cook over low to medium heat until onion is translucent. While that's cooking, strain the giblet broth. Discard the neck and vegetables. *Save the broth!* Chop the giblets into ¼-inch pieces and add to the onion and celery mixture. Remove from heat. Add 4 tablespoons fresh rubbed sage. (A little goes a long way, so be careful not to go overboard.)

Pour mixture into bread pieces and stir well to mix. Add 1 cup at a time of giblet broth to the mixture and stir well until dressing "clumps" and stays together when a small amount is pressed together with your fingers. For this amount of dressing, I usually use about 2 to 3 cups of broth. It may seem less moist than you want your finished product, but it will also absorb juice from the turkey as it cooks and you don't want soggy, pasty stuffing. *Save the remaining broth!* You're now ready to stuff the turkey.

When cooking a turkey that is 18 pounds or more, allow about 15 minutes per pound; if below 18 pounds, allow about 20 to 25 minutes per pound. When you've figured out how much time the turkey needs in the oven, add one hour to the front end for making the dressing and stuffing the bird and one hour to the other end for 30 minutes of "rest" time when it comes out of the oven. You'll need another 30 minutes for carving. If you figure 5 hours of cooking time, you'll need to start to make the dressing 7 hours before you want to sit down at the table.

Preheat the oven to 450 degrees. Make sure you have a large clean surface on which to work. Place turkey on surface so the neck cavity is facing upward. Cut a large piece of cheesecloth, open to a single thickness and place in neck cavity to form a lining. Fill with dressing; pack lightly. If you pack too much in the cavity it will become soggy and dense. Twirl end of the cheesecloth to close and tuck inside to keep it secured. Because the cloth will contain the dressing, you can fill so that it exceeds the cavity and protrudes from the turkey. Stretch neck skin over dressing and secure with skewers. (Mom used to sew it shut with a heavy thread and a darning needle.) Turn the turkey over and repeat the process in the large cavity. Use a very large piece of cheesecloth. In this size of a turkey, you should be able to get the remaining dressing in to this large cavity by allowing it to protrude and be contained by the cloth. Secure the legs in place with the metal holder that comes with the bird or tie the legs together. Twist the cheesecloth to close the bag and tuck inside to secure. Place the turkey on a rack in a large roasting pan.

Cover the wing tips with aluminum foil to keep them from burning. Cut a piece of cheesecloth large enough to cover the top of the turkey; it helps to hold the butter on the surface and will still allow it to brown. Melt 1 cup of butter in a small saucepan and brush on turkey so the cheesecloth is completely saturated. Place a large piece of aluminum foil over turkey and press to conform to its shape. This prevents the turkey from getting too brown too fast.

Turn the oven down to 300 degrees and place turkey in oven. Set timer and baste every 30 minutes. Remove the aluminum foil for the last 30 minutes. A turkey this size will take approximately 5 hours in the oven or 15 minutes per pound. Besides checking with a reliable thermometer, you can also hold onto the drumstick with a towel and twist. If it rocks easily in the joint, it's finished. The turkey must sit for another 30 minutes before you can even think about carving, and it will continue to cook while it is resting. This "rest" allows the juices to be redistributed throughout the meat. And *no picking* while you and your guests wait for it to be carved!

When the carver begins, I pull the dressing "bags" from the turkey and set them in their serving dishes covered with aluminum foil until we're ready to sit down. It keeps the dressing hot.

I usually serve just two vegetables with dinner, but I have included several here so you have some choice.

Thyme Corn

15-ounce can white corn or 16-ounce bag frozen corn (yellow works fine, but I prefer white)
1 tablespoon butter or margarine
¾ teaspoon dried thyme, or 1 teaspoon fresh
2 teaspoons fresh lemon juice

Sauté corn in butter, add thyme and lemon juice and simmer until heated and flavors have a time to blend. This recipe serves 4. I'd double or triple this recipe if you are serving only one other vegetable. If it's your only veggie, quadruple it.

Mushrooms and Celery

5 stalks of celery (each stalk equals about 1 cup), washed and sliced into thin diagonal pieces
½ pound fresh mushrooms, washed and sliced
2 tablespoons margarine, melted (or spray a larg skillet with an oil spray such as Pam)
¼ to ½ cup Italian salad dressing such as Good Season's

Melt butter in a large skillet and add mushrooms and celery. Stir until mushrooms are soft; celery should still be crisp. Add just enough Italian dressing to coat lightly. Stir until hot and serve. This recipe will serve four if you are serving two veggies. As with the corn, I'd double if serving one other vegetable.

Steamed Broccoli

2 heads fresh broccoli
1 tablespoon butter or margarine (optional)
juice of ½ lemon

Fresh broccoli, washed and broken into small pieces and steamed is an easy veggie to do. Of course, you can always serve frozen but I think that fresh is always the best and doesn't really take much longer to prepare.

Steam in a vegetable steamer until done to desired crispness or mushiness. You can also put into a large pan with about an inch of water and cook over medium heat until done. Put in serving dish and, if desired, dab with pieces of margarine or butter and squeeze half a fresh lemon over the top.

This recipe serves 4. If serving double recipes of the other two, I'd make one serving of broccoli.

All of these vegetables can be prepared while the turkey is roasting and simply warmed on the stove or reheated in the microwave right before table time.

Mashed Potatoes and Gravy

8 potatoes peeled and cut into small pieces
2 tablespoons butter or margarine
4 ounces cream cheese, regular or light
½ cup milk
salt
garlic powder (optional)

Double this recipe for 16 guests.

This recipe can be done ahead of time and reheated, but I like to do it within an hour or so of the turkey coming out of the oven. When the turkey comes out, the potatoes go into the oven (350 degrees) until you are ready to serve. If you make them the day before, you need to have two ovens or plan to leave the turkey sit for longer than 30 minutes while you reheat the potatoes in a 350-degree oven for about 45 to 60 minutes You can also put into a microwave-safe bowl and reheat.

We like to have leftover mashed potatoes, so I take that into account when peeling. Figure on one medium potato per guest plus whatever you want for Saturday night's repeat of the dinner. Cut potatoes into small pieces and place in a large pan, cover with water. Add a pinch or two of salt, depending on the quantity, and cover with a lid. Bring to boil, uncover (or it will boil over), and simmer until a fork is easily inserted but not mushy. *Pour the water into another container and save for the gravy!*

For 8 medium potatoes boiled and drained and placed in a large mixing bowl, add margarine and beat with mixer until the big lumps are gone

Add cream cheese; mix until blended. Add small amounts of milk, about ¼ cup at a time, and mix until you have the creamy texture that your family enjoys. I don't add any salt and pepper but go for it if you wish. You can also add a pinch of garlic powder if you like a garlicky flavor. The cream cheese gives them "body" so the consistency doesn't change when they are reheated.

Place potatoes in an ovenproof or microwave-safe dish and cover with foil until it is time to reheat. This dish can be made the day before but if you do, cover and refrigerate. Serves 8.

Gravy

turkey pan drippings
giblet broth and potato water
1½ cup flour, for thickening
salt and fresh ground pepper, to taste
chicken broth (may not be needed)

This is where I usually hear moaning and gnashing of teeth. There are several ways to make the thickening. Mom would put about 1½ cups of flour into a 4-cup measuring cup and add small amounts of water and blend until there was a ball of paste. Then she worked the paste until all of the lumps were gone and added water until it had the consistency of cream soup.

An alternative is to put about 1 cup of flour and 1 cup of water into a jar with a tight lid and shake the heck out of it until you have a smooth product. I have had equal success with both...and equal failures. If you end up with a lumpy product, just put it through a sieve to rid the

thickening of the pesky lumps and forge ahead. The gravy thickening can be made anytime after the turkey is in the oven so that it's ready and waiting.

As soon as the turkey is taken out of the oven, lift it to the platter or cutting board where it will "rest" for the next 30 minutes. My husband uses two clean towels to lift the bird from the pan. Be careful! That turkey is HOT! Remove as much of the grease from the pan as possible. You can pour it off carefully, use a large spoon to skim it off, or use anyone of the handy gadgets that are on the market now for separating the good meat juice from the fat.

You want at least 8 cups of liquid for the gravy. Combine the giblet broth and potato water and measure. If necessary, add chicken broth to make 8 cups. (If you have more than 8 cups, save it for a minute until you read the rest of the paragraph.) There should be a lot of rich, dark drippings and meat juice left in the bottom of the pan. Add the 8 cups of liquid and turn on the heat. If the pan spans two burners on your stove, turn them both to high. Use a fork to scrape all of the "goodies" from the bottom of the pan. This large turkey could make more than 8 cups of gravy so if you want more, just add the extra liquid, one cup at a time, tasting after each addition to make sure that adding another cup wouldn't dilute the rich taste. I always make as much of this rich broth as the drippings will allow.

If you don't need all of the gravy for today's meal (and one other leftover meal to be consumed in the next day or two), now is the time to take 2 to 3 cups of the rich broth and freeze it to make at a later time. Gravy doesn't freeze well, but there is a great way to have good gravy at a later date. Just make a little thickening, bring the broth to a boil in a saucepan, and follow the directions for adding the thickening.

When there is a rolling boil, very slowly pour in the gravy thickening while stirring as fast as you can. This is the secret to "lumpless" gravy. Continue to add the thickening until you have the desired consistency—you may not need all of it. If you run out before it's as thick as you want it to be, just give it another minute or two on high heat to see if it thickens more. If not, turn off the burners, make a little more thickening, turn the heat back on, and get the rolling boil going again and pick up where you left off. Salt and pepper to taste. If you've taken all of the precautions and still get lumps, just run the gravy through a sieve as you pour it into the gravy boats right before serving. No one will know if you can keep everyone out of the kitchen!

Rolls

There are many choices. The easiest, of course, is to buy readymade rolls and heat them before dinner is served. I don't recommend putting them in the microwave as they get rubbery. Preheat oven to 350 degrees. I like to put them in large, brown paper bag, sprinkle with a little water. Turn oven off and put rolls in for about 5 minutes.

A second choice is a good old standby from the dairy case: crescent rolls or biscuits. Simply follow the directions on the package and put them into the oven so they are the last thing you do before sitting down to the table.

I like to make the rolls "fresh" from the Pillsbury Hot Roll Mix box. There are a number of similar products on the market that are good. Make the dough according to the directions on the box after the turkey goes into the oven. Let the dough rise, form into rolls, and cover with a towel until it's time to put them into oven. You'll put them in the oven after the turkey comes out. Serve with butter.

Pumpkin Pie With Whipped Cream

We like to clear the table and sit with a good cup of coffee and let everything settle for a while before having dessert. I recommend you have your guests bring the pies. Whether they really mean it or not, most people ask what they can bring. Give yourself a break and take them up on their offer! You'll have you hands full getting the rest of the dinner on the table on time. If there are no guests coming to your feast, then buy the pies from your favorite pie shop. But if you must make everything on your table, then I recommend you make my mom's "Punkin Pie."

readymade unbaked piecrust
15-ounce can Libby's cooked pumpkin
12-ounce can evaporated whole milk
2 eggs
¾ cup sugar
¼ teaspoon ground ginger
½ teaspoon each allspice, cinnamon, nutmeg, and cloves

Use a ready-made piecrust found in the dairy case at the market. I like those that are not in a pan already but are prerolled pastry dough you put into your own pan. A 15-ounce can will make one pie; a 26-ounce can will make two.

Use about ¼ teaspoon each of ginger, ½ teaspoon allspice, cinnamon, nutmeg, and cloves, per pie. Mix together the pumpkin, sugar, spices followed by the milk. Beat the eggs separately and then fold in last. Bake at 425 degrees for about 10 minutes then turn down to 325 degrees and bake until a clean table knife inserted into the middle gently comes out clean, about 40 to 55 minutes. Remove from oven and sit on racks to cool. This recipe makes 1 pie. If making two pies, use only 1 can evaporated milk and use regular milk (just fill the evaporated can to measure) for the rest.

Whipped Cream

Of course, you can buy readymade whipped cream in the can, but I like to make my own.

1½ cups whipping cream
1½ teaspoons sugar, to taste
1 teaspoon vanilla

Whip the cream with the sugar, until soft peaks form. Add vanilla and beat until peaks are firm. (Don't over-beat or you'll have very sweet butter!) Put a dollop on each serving of pie.

The cream will whip faster if you use a cold bowl and beaters. Just put them in the freezer before you sit down to dinner.

Now for the finishing touches of your dinner! Purchase a can of cranberry sauce. Take the lid off of one end, use a beer can opener or ice pick to make a hole in the other end to release the vacuum and the sauce will slide out in one piece. Cut sauce into thin slices.

Put black olives into serving dish. Pour the beverages—wine, milk, juice, water. Make a fresh pot of coffee and turn it on right before you sit down so it's ready to serve once the table is cleared of all the food. Sit down and enjoy!

Timetable

1 week to 10 days before Thanksgiving:

· Order a fresh turkey or buy a frozen one. If you have purchased a frozen turkey, begin to thaw according to the instructions. Remember you will need about 5 or 6 days to defrost a turkey of this size in the refrigerator. It would be a real problem if it were still frozen when you're trying to get those giblets out the day before Thanksgiving!

A few days before:

· Do the grocery shopping. (Don't do it too soon. You want the perishables to be fresh)

1 day before:

· Remove the giblets from the turkey and make the giblet broth.
· Clean turkey of pin feathers, wash, dry, and cover; refrigerate.
· Early in the day, spread the bread out to dry.
· Late in day or evening, break bread into tiny pieces; leave uncovered overnight.
· Chop onions and celery for the dressing.
· Make the Pumpkin Pie if your guests are not bringing dessert.
· Set table.
· Decide which serving dishes you need and polish, if necessary.

Thanksgiving Day:

The following timetable is for a 15- to 20-pound turkey that needs to be in the oven for about 5 hours and rest for 30 minutes. The timetable works for this wide range because cooking times are longer for a turkey under 18 pounds. Smaller turkeys actually take about 20 minutes per pound.

8 hours before dinner (6½ hours if cooking a 10- to 11-pound turkey):
· Take turkey out of the refrigerator.

7 hours before (5½ hours if cooking a 10- to 11-pound turkey):
· Make dressing and stuff the bird.

6½ hours before (5 hours if cooking a 10- to 11-pound turkey):
· Preheat oven to 450 degrees.

6 hours before (4½ hours if cooking a 10- to 11-pound turkey):
· Put turkey in oven and turn oven down to 300 degrees.
· Set the timer every 30 minutes to baste the bird. By the time that all of the butter is gone, you can begin to use the drippings in the bottom of the pan.

During the next 2½ to 3 hours:
· Make the gravy thickening and set aside.
· Put cranberry sauce and black olives into

their serving dishes, cover with plastic wrap, and refrigerate.

- Prepare vegetables. If doing the corn and/or mushrooms and celery, you can complete preparation and reheat before dinner. If doing broccoli, clean and cut but don't steam yet unless you want mushy broccoli.
- Peel potatoes, cover with water, and add a pinch or 2 of salt. (If you made them yesterday, it's now time to take them out of the refrigerator and allow them to warm to room temperature.)
- If making rolls from a box, prepare dough, shape rolls, cover with a towel, and set aside.
- Toward the end of this time, boil potatoes, mash, and cover with aluminum foil. Put them in an ovenproof dish. Transfer to a serving dish when they are reheated. I put them inside the microwave because I think it helps keep them warm.
- Put butter on serving dish and place back in the refrigerator.
- Prepare the coffeemaker so all you have to do later is turn it on. Grind beans and set aside for a second pot.

2 to 2½ hours before:

- Take some time for yourself. Soak in a hot tub or lie down for a minute or two before getting dressed.

1½ hours before (guest begin to arrive):

- Prepare Jalapeño Jelly Over Cream Cheese

With Crackers and serve. Offer a beverage.

1 hour before:

- Take the turkey out of the oven.
- Turn up oven to 350 degrees and immediately put potatoes in to heat.
- Put the turkey on the cutting board or platter. *No picking!*
- Remove fat from roasting pan and make gravy.

30 minutes before (People are always asking if there is anything they can do to help. Now is the time to take them up on their offer!):

- Have someone else begin to carve the turkey (but only if they won't do a hatchet job on it).
- Put the dressing bags into the serving dishes and cover with foil to keep hot.
- Start reheating veggies in the microwave.
- If serving broccoli, turn on burner and steam.
- Put cranberries, olives, and butter on the table.
- Put rolls in oven to bake; assign someone to watch them or set the timer.
- Pour beverages.
- Light candles.

10 minutes before:

- Put all hot food, including the turkey, in serving dishes and put on the table.
- Take dressing out of cheesecloth and put

into serving dish.

- Pour gravy into gravy boats and put on table.
- Take rolls out of oven, put in basket, and place on table.
- Turn on coffeemaker.
- Call your guests to the table!

- When people are served, make a toast to good friends, the bounty of good food, and the universe for bringing both together in the holiday spirit!

Shopping List

Check your pantry for these staples. Add those you are missing to your shopping list. Consider the amounts you'll be preparing. If you stick with my menu, you'll need the following from the supermarket. Add in the amounts based on the whether you will double or triple a recipe.

___coffee
___fresh cracked pepper
___salt
___ground cloves
___cinnamon
___thyme
___rubbed sage
___ginger
___nutmeg
___allspice
___bay leaf
___vanilla
___sugar
___flour
___chicken broth

Here's what you'll need to add to your weekly shopping list:
___tom turkey
___eggs (pumpkin pie)
___cream cheese (appetizer, mashed potatoes)
___milk (mashed potatoes, pumpkin pie)
___butter or margarine (dressing, mashed potatoes, broccoli, basting turkey, corn, mushrooms and celery, rolls)
___whipped cream (pumpkin pie)
___potatoes (mashed potatoes)
___onions (giblet broth, dressing)

___carrot (giblet broth)
___celery (giblet broth, mushrooms and celery*, dressing)
___broccoli*
___mushrooms* (mushrooms and celery)
___lemons (broccoli, corn)
___corn*
___Libby's canned pumpkin (pumpkin pie)
___evaporated milk (pumpkin pie)
___cranberry sauce
___bread (dressing)
___dinner roll mix or readymade rolls
___crackers (appetizers)
___pie crust (pumpkin pie)
___black olives
___Good Season's Italian salad dressing (mushrooms and celery)
___jalapeño jelly (appetizer)
___mixed nuts (appetizer, optional)
___aluminum foil (turkey)
___cheese cloth (dressing, turkey)
___candles
___sparkling cider
___wine

*Cross these items off or reduce amount if you've chosen different veggies for side dishes.

Shopping List Amounts

The amounts on your shopping list will depend on how many you are serving for dinner. For 8 people, you'll need 2 vegetable servings of 4; for 12, you'll need 3 servings of 4; and for 16, you'll need 4 servings of 4.

To Serve:	8	12	16
tom turkey	10 to 11 lbs	15 to 16 lbs	20 to 22 lbs
eggs	2	4	4
cream cheese	12 oz	14 oz	16 oz
milk	½ cup	2 1/4 cups	2½ cups
butter or margarine	2 lbs	2 lbs	2 lbs
whipped cream	½ pint	1 pint	1 pint
potatoes	8 plus	12 plus	16 plus
onions	3 medium	3 medium	4 medium
carrots	1	1	1
celery	1 bunch	1 bunch	1 bunch
broccoli	4 large heads	6 large heads	8 large heads
mushrooms	1 lb	1½ lbs	2 lbs
lemons	1	2	3
corn	2 15-oz cans	3 15-oz cans	4 15-oz cans
Libby's canned pumpkin	1 15-oz can	1 26-oz can	1 26-oz can
evaporated milk	1 12-oz can	1 12-oz can	1 12-oz can
cranberry sauce	1 15-oz can	2 15-oz cans	2 15-oz cans
bread	1 loaf	1 loaf	1 1/2 loaf
dinner roll mix or readymade rolls	1 mix (12 rolls)	1 mix (12 rolls)	2 mixes (16 rolls)
crackers	1 box	1 box	1 box
pie crust	1 package of 2	1 package of 2	1 package of 2
black olives	1 15-oz can	1 15-oz can	1 15-oz can
Good Season's Italian salad dressing	1 package	1 package	1 package
jalapeño jelly	1 8-oz jar	1 8-oz jar	1 8-oz jar
mixed nuts	1 1-lb can	1 1-lb can	1 1-lb can
aluminum foil	1 roll	1 roll	1 roll
cheese cloth	1 package	1 package	1 package
candles	2 (minimum)	4 (minimum)	4 (minimum)
sparkling cider wine	1 bottle for every two people, depending on number of drinkers and nondrinkers		

BUFFET DINNER FOR TWENTY-FIVE: SPECIAL HOLIDAY

Shrimp Cocktail
Crab Delight
Vegetable Tray and Dip
Baked Brie With Almonds
Spiced Nuts
Prime Rib
Turkey Breast
Scalloped Potatoes
Cucumber Salad
Ambrosia
Rolls
Dessert

Hanukkah, Christmas, and New Year's are a very special time of year. Even if we don't do much entertaining the rest of the year, many of us find the courage to volunteer to host the office party or family get-togethers. As usual, food brings the whole event together. A buffet is a great way to entertain because it allows you to do most of the work up front and then enjoy time with your guests.

There are many options to this type of party. If you and your friends are fairly casual, you can assign each one to bring a particular dish. You furnish the dishes and drinks. Or have your guests bring the appetizers and desserts, and you furnish the rest. But if you want to do everything yourself, this menu will easily serve 25 guests. When preparing for a group this large, I try to include some holiday favorites but keep it as simple as possible.

I usually plan for the party to start with appetizers and cocktails around 7 o'clock and serve dinner at eight or so. Make sure you put this information on the invitation so your guests understand that dinner is being served and it is not an open house.

If your home lends itself to this, serve your drinks and appetizers near the kitchen/family room area. This keeps people from setting used plates and glasses on the dining room table where you will be setting up the buffet. There is nothing worse than having a guest spill something on your beautiful table before you even get started. It also allows you to be a part of the activity while you complete the preparations for dinner. I have found that select guests are often interested in giving a helping hand and this arrangement encourages it. If you are in an apartment, consider serving the "starters" on the patio area or in the living room, but away from the dining table.

Planning. Most people decorate their house for the holidays anyway, so there is little extra that you have to do. I put all of the extensions in the dining room table and use my black tablecloth. If you want this to be a "nondenominational" party, you can use any color and numbers of candles in the arrangement. Place large bows on your tallest candleholders and allow the streamers to be intertwined around the base of the candles. Fill space at the bottom of the candlestick holders with tiny curls of metallic ribbon.

If you want a Christmas centerpiece, consider using a crimson tablecloth and four sets of compatible candlestick holders of various heights, several oil-filled candles, and a few votives in a cluster to make up the majority of the centerpiece. Place four different-sized mauve and crimson Christmas balls on four of the candleholders at different heights and mauve candles in the remaining holders. Silk poinsettias and a dozen or more Christmas balls interspersed among the base of the candles complete the arrangement.

Another simple but beautiful arrangement is a crystal bowl filled with an assortment of Christmas ornaments, flanked by candles. Or place evergreen boughs down the center of the table and tall or votive candles and Christmas ornaments among the greens.

For Hannukah, use silver and blue ribbons and candles, and place dreidles and gelt (chocolate covered in gold to resemble coins) among the curled ribbons. For New Year's, I like to use ivory candles and gold ribbon.

Planning the amount of food for a large group can feel like a guessing game. I usually end up with too much. I have found that substantial appetizers guarantee the main course will stretch to accommodate a larger-than-expected turnout. Add a few desserts and no one will go away hungry.

The following appetizers will easily serve at least 25. If you feel that you need more, add another ½ pound of shrimp and a few more veggies. Serve with wine, beer, soft drinks, or mixed drinks.

Shrimp Cocktail

1½ pounds cleaned and deveined shrimp
Cocktail Sauce

One to 1½ pounds of shrimp, served with cocktail sauce, will be more than enough. Of course, you can get raw shrimp, place in boiling water for approximately 2 minutes until they turn pink and quickly place into strainer and rinse with cold water to stop the cooking process. Peel and devein and place in refrigerator until serving. The cooking and cleaning will take at least 1 hour. I suggest you purchase frozen, cleaned, cooked shrimp from the frozen food section. Often this is what you can buy in the "fresh" fish case at the market, but it will cost you several dollars a pound for them to open the bag and run cold water over them to defrost the tasty little treats. To defrost, place in colander and let cold water run over shrimp for a few minutes. Let them sit, periodically running water over them until thawed. If you're in a hurry, run water over them until totally defrosted. Refrigerate until use.

Cocktail Sauce

2 cups ketchup
2 tablespoons fresh lemon juice
2 teaspoons Worcestershire sauce
white horseradish, to taste

If your horseradish has been in the refrigerator for over one month, you should buy a new jar—it looses its punch quickly. Combine the first three ingredients and then add the horseradish to taste. Start by adding 1 tablespoon, mix well, and taste. Continue to add small amounts until it has the desired zip.

Or you can buy readymade sauce, often found in the cheese and lunchmeat case at the store.

Baked Brie With Almonds

1 round of Brie cheese, about 5 to 6 inches in diameter
½ cup sliced almonds
2 tablespoons butter or margarine
crackers and/or French bread

At least 1 hour before serving time, remove Brie from refrigerator and allow it to come to room temperature. Melt butter in small skillet and add almonds and sauté over low heat. Stir frequently, keeping a close eye on them as they can burn easily. Remove from heat when toasted lightly.

About 10 minutes before you wish to serve the Brie, place on a microwave-safe dish and microwave on high heat for 30 seconds, turn, and let sit for about a minute. Continue to microwave in 30-second "spurts" with brief rest periods in between until Brie puffs and center is very soft. The trick is to do it slowly so the outer rind does not split, causing the melted cheese to run all over the plate. It usually takes about 2 to 2½ minutes total to get the middle hot and bubbly. If the almonds have cooled, reheat quickly (don't let them get too brown), spread on top of cheese, and serve with crackers or thin slices of French bread.

If you don't wish to use a microwave, place cheese on an ovenproof dish and place in a 350-degree oven for about 20 minutes until the cheese is hot and the center puffs a bit.

Crab Delight

(courtesy of Kathie Davis)

12 ounces soft cream cheese
1 tablespoon Worcestershire sauce
2 teaspoons onion, finely chopped (You can substitute dried minced onions that have been reconstituted according to the instructions on the jar, with all excess water removed.)
½ cup or so bottled cocktail chili sauce (If you are serving the shrimp appetizer and making your own cocktail sauce, make another ½ cup for this dish at the same time.)
6-ounce can crab meat or fresh, separated into small pieces
dried parsley

Mix cream cheese, lemon juice, onions, and Worcestershire sauce together and spread as the bottom layer in an attractive 9-inch pie or ceramic tart dish. Spread about ½ to ¾ cup cocktail sauce to cover cream cheese completely. Sprinkle sauce with crab and garnish with dried parsley. Cover with plastic wrap and refrigerate until use. Serve with crackers.

Tip: If it's available, try jicama for your veggie tray. It's mild, crisp, and great for dipping!

Spiced Nuts

1 pound whole almonds, pecans, or mixed, unsalted nuts
4 tablespoons butter or margarine
1 teaspoon cinnamon
½ teaspoon sugar
½ teaspoon nutmeg
¼ teaspoon cloves

Mix together spices. In a large skillet, melt butter, add nuts, and toast until lightly brown. Remove from heat and stir in spices to coat nuts.

This recipe can be made ahead of time and stored in an airtight container for up to a week. The nuts can also be frozen immediately and brought out in small batches as needed. They defrost quickly so they can be kept on hand for drop-in guests.

Variation: Substitute spices above with ½ teaspoon garlic salt, ½ teaspoon curry, and ¼ to ½ teaspoon cayenne pepper, depending on how spicy you like it. Or add 1 teaspoon Worcestershire sauce to the melted butter and follow the rest of the recipe, as above.

Vegetable Tray and Dip

raw vegetables, such as celery, carrots, peppers, cucumbers and mushrooms, washed and cut into small dipping pieces
1 pint sour cream (regular, lowfat, or nonfat)
1 package Lipton onion soup mix

Fill a large serving tray with your favorite vegetables. If you want to save time, spend a little extra and buy veggies that are already cut. (You can also purchase readymade dip—but remember to put it into one of your own decorative bowls.) Mix together onion soup mix and sour cream.

Prime Rib

10 to 12 pounds deboned (5 ribs) prime rib roast
3 garlic cloves
salt
fresh ground pepper

About a week before the party, order a deboned prime rib from the butcher. You may also want to try the meat section of your regular grocery store, where it will cost substantially less. I've found excellent roasts there and at the local food warehouse store, such as Costco and Sam's.

Amounts are always tricky. Each rib is worth about 2 to 2½ pounds and will feed 3 to 4 people. If you are having a variety of appetizers and also serving a roasted turkey breast, you can probably stretch that to 5 to 6 people per rib.

There are as many ways to roast prime rib as there are cookbooks. Over the years, I have finally settled on this method: Take the meat out of the refrigerator at least an hour before you plan to put it in the oven and let it sit, covered on the counter. Preheat oven to 500 degrees.

In the meantime, peel the garlic and cut each into about four pieces. With a small paring knife, make a deep cut, pushing it into the meat to the hilt of the knife, remove the knife. and then press your finger into the cut to expand the hole. Immediately push in a piece of the garlic. Do the same with the remaining garlic, evenly distributing throughout the roast. Sprinkle the outside of the roast with salt and fresh ground pepper, pressing it into the meat.

How long to roast the meat is a guessing game because it will vary with the size of the roast, the oven, the temperature of the roast when it goes in the oven, and the accuracy of the oven thermometer. In general, I usually go for medium rare—a warm, pink center. The ends will be less pink for those who like theirs a little more done and those who like theirs rare can be appeased by a pinker center. Figure about 18 to 20 minutes per pound. A thermometer placed in the center of the roast (never resting in fat or on bone) should read 160 degrees right before it is carved.

For a rare roast, figure about 15 to 18 minutes and 140 degrees. If you insist on cooking it to death, with no pink in the middle, it will take anywhere from 25 to 30 minutes per pound to ruin it! (No bias here!) The thermometer will read 170 degrees or above.

As with a turkey, the roast will need to "rest" for 20 to 30 minutes before it is carved. This allows the juices from the center of the roast to be redistributed to the outer edge. Remember it will continue to cook even after it is out of the oven so consider that when figuring when to take the roast out of the oven. Remove it when it is 10 degrees shy of the desired inner temperature. As soon as I take it out, I always make a small cut into the very center to check its status. If it is already perfect, then I break my own rule of letting it rest, and carve it immediately, which will stop the cooking process. I slice it as thin as possible and cover the platter with aluminum foil to keep it hot. You will lose a great deal of the juice to the bottom of the platter, but I find this more acceptable than overcooked meat! For medium rare, I usually pull the roast out of the oven when the thermometer reads 150 degrees.

You will need to decide, at least the day before the party, how long your roast needs to be in the oven. Make sure you ask the butcher to write the weight on the package or save the label so you have the exact number of pounds. Place the roast in the preheated oven to 500 degrees and immediately turn it down to 325 degrees. Allow it to roast and try not to open the oven door until you are about a half hour from the time you *think* you should be taking it out of the oven. Check the thermometer to determine how close you are to being on schedule. There have been times when I have had to pull the roast out immediately in order to allow its rest period. At other times, I find I have to extend the roasting time by at least another half hour. There have even been times when I have had to carve it immediately. After carving, garnish platter with fresh parsley. If you are not quite ready to serve, cover with foil and hold the parsley until you are ready to place the meat on the table.

Turkey Breast

Because there are many people who do not eat red meat, you may want to think about serving a turkey breast as well. If you do so, you can decrease the size of the roast by 1 rib. Consider buying a breast that is precooked. Smoked turkey breast tastes very similar to ham. They will often come spiral cut and do not even need to be reheated, which will actually dry out the meat. This is helpful if you have limited oven space and other things that need to go in to the oven after the roast comes out.

2 to 3 pounds roasted turkey breast

Scalloped Potatoes

I like to make mine from scratch but when pushed for time, I have used the "boxed" variety. They are very tasty and only take a few minutes to assemble.

Figure about 4 medium potatoes for 5 to 6 servings. Peel and slice very thin (a food processor or hand slicer can shorten the process). For every 4 potatoes, figure the following:
1 tablespoon flour
½ cup diced onion

1 teaspoon salt
½ teaspoon dry mustard
½ teaspoon thyme
fresh ground pepper, to taste
2 tablespoons butter or margarine
1½ cup milk or cream (cream makes for a much richer although "fatter" dish)

Grease a 9- by 13-inch baking dish with margarine. Depending on how many potatoes you use, you may need to use an additional 8- by 8-inch casserole.

Place several layers of potatoes in the dish, dot with margarine, and sprinkle with flour and some of the onions. Continue layering until all potatoes and onions are used. Dot last layer with butter only (no flour).

Mix together dry mustard, salt, thyme, and pepper, and add to the milk or cream. Pour over potatoes. Liquid should come at least ¾ of the way up the sides. Add a little more milk or cream if necessary to reach that mark.

Cover with aluminum foil to prevent burning. Bake at 350 for about 45 minutes or until potatoes are soft. Check after 30 minutes and remove foil to brown the top a little, if necessary. You can bake this earlier in the day and reheat in the microwave before serving, or pop back in the oven at 350 degrees for about 20 to 25 minutes to reheat. If you're going to go the microwave route, make sure you dishes will fit in the microwave.

Ambrosia

1 15-ounce can mandarin oranges, drained
1 15-ounce can pineapple chunks
same amount miniature marshmallows (use
one of the above cans to measure)
same amount shredded coconut
1 cup sour cream

People really seem to enjoy this side dish, and it is very easy to make a day ahead of time. For this crowd though, with all of the other food, I would just double the recipe. Combine the following:

Place drained mandarin oranges and pineapple into a large bowl. Add coconut and miniature marshmallows. Add sour cream and mix well. (Add a little more sour cream if needed to make a salad that is "bound" but not soggy.) Cover and refrigerate until serving time. Serves 8.

Tip: Miniature marshmallows freeze well. Keep them on hand and defrost as needed.

Cucumber Salad

This salad is great for summer picnics too.
1 ounce thin bean or rice stick noodles
3 cups water
6 large cucumbers
2 large garlic cloves, minced very, very fine
1 teaspoon sugar
1 tablespoon rice vinegar (or white vinegar)
3 tablespoons soy sauce
1 teaspoon sesame seed oil
Chili Oil, to taste

Place about 1 ounce of noodles into boiling water (Just "eye-ball" how much 1 ounce is based on the size of the package. The exact amount here isn't crucial.) and let sit while you prepare the rest of the salad.

Peel the equivalent of six large cucumbers, cut in half lengthwise and scoop out seeds with a teaspoon. Slice lengthwise again and cut into ¼-inch pieces. Place in a large bowl. Drain the noodles in a colander or sieve and cut into lengths of about 1 to 1-½ inches. Add, along with other ingredients, to bowl and stir well. Cover and refrigerate until serving time.

Chili Oil

Of course you can purchase this in the Oriental food section at the grocery store, but it is easy to make yourself.
½ cup peanut or vegetable oil
¼ cup sesame oil
½ cup dried red pepper flakes
1 tablespoon cayenne pepper

Heat peanut or vegetable oil and sesame oil over a medium heat until a pepper flake sizzles when added. Carefully add red pepper flakes to oil; it may boil over. Remove from heat, add cayenne pepper. Cover and let sit overnight. Strain into a jar. Cover with a tight lid and refrigerate. Will keep for months.

Rolls

Refer to page 8 in the Thanksgiving section. For a crowd this size, I heartily recommend you serve store-bought rolls. Or use a box mix and make them several weeks ahead of time and freeze. Defrost the morning of the party and reheat right before serving.

Dessert

If you are doing all of the work yourself, you have your hands full with the appetizers and main course. For dessert, check out the freezer section at your grocery store. There are many wonderful desserts available. Or go to your favorite pie shop. This will save you hours of time.

If you are on close terms with your guests, instead of serving traditional desserts, you can ask everyone to bring a dozen holiday cookies. You'll end up with a great assortment of treats that will top off your wonderful meal. I find that people often don't have room for a large dessert but do like to finish the meal on a sweet note and a cup of good coffee.

Tip: On a slow day, think about the holiday meals or other special occasions that may be coming up in the next 6 to 8 months. If you are like many families, you have standard meals that you prepare for these meals. Make a list of the nonperishable foods that you use in these meals and watch for them to turn up on specials at the market. Not only do you save money but also it spreads the cost of these meals throughout the year.

Timetable

1 week before event:
· Order roast and turkey breast.

Several days before:
· If you don't need to use your table between now and the party, decorate the table and set out the china, crystal, and flatware. (For casual gatherings, you can certainly use paper plates and plastic utensils, but use plastic or heavy paper dinner plates that won't get soggy.)

1 day before:
· Make cocktail sauce and refrigerate.
· Prepare spiced nuts and store in an airtight container.
· Prepare veggies and dip. Place veggies in Ziploc bags. Make dip in sour cream container. Refrigerate.
· Prepare cream cheese layer for crab appetizer and refrigerate. This must be assembled the day of the party so the color from the cocktail sauce doesn't "run."
· If you don't need the space, set up the bar/beverage area.
· Mix together all ingredients for the ambrosia *except* the sour cream; that will be done before serving so it doesn't get "watery."
· Figure out how long the roast needs to be in the oven and make out your schedule

for the day of the party.
· Decide which serving dishes and platters you will use for all of the food and polish, if necessary.

In the morning on the day of the party:
· Decorate and set the table.
· Set up the beverage area.
· Defrost shrimp; refrigerate.
· Assemble Crab Delight; refrigerate.
· Make scalloped potatoes and bake; you can reheat them in the microwave or put them in the oven when the roast comes out.
· Drain and discard the excess juice and add sour cream to ambrosia; place in serving dish and refrigerate.
· Make cucumber salad and place in serving dish; refrigerate.
· Place butter on serving dish; refrigerate.
· If you baked rolls ahead of time, take out of freezer to thaw.

5¼ hours before the roast is put on the dining room table:
(This schedule is for a 12-pound roast that needs 3½ hours plus the 30-minute rest period. If you're making a smaller roast, adjust this process to allow for the shorter roasting time. Figure out how much *less* time it will take for the meat to roast and simply subtract it from 6¼ hours. For example, if the roast is only 8 pounds, it will take about 3 hours including the resting

time, so you would pull the meat out of the refrigerator 5¼ hours before putting it on the table. The rest of the schedule can be changed by the same amount of time with the exception of the time for you. You'll have to slot that in about 4 hours before serving time so you're available to preheat the oven and put the roast in on schedule. Of course, if you have helpers, you can instruct them to preheat the oven, turn down the temperature, and put the roast in.)

· Remove roast from refrigerator and prepare it with garlic and pepper.

4¾ hours before dinner:
· Preheat oven to 500 degrees.

4¼ hours before:
· Turn oven down to 325 degrees and put meat into the oven.

4 hours:
· Take time for yourself to rest a moment and get dressed.

2 hours before dinner and 1 hour before guests begin to arrive:
· Prepare first pot of coffee but don't turn on yet.
· Grind coffee beans for two more pots of coffee and place in filters; set aside.
· Place veggies on tray, put dip into serving

dish, and return to refrigerator.
· Take Brie out of refrigerator, remove wrapping, and place on microwave-safe serving dish.

1½ hours before:
· Melt butter and toast almond for the Brie.
· Slice bread and place along with crackers in serving basket or dish.

1¼ hours before:
· Complete beverage setup—open wine, fill ice bucket, and so forth.
· Check roast with thermometer. It should come out of the oven when it is about 10 degrees from the desired finished temperature. If already at that temperature, pull out and allow resting. You'll just carve it a little sooner, place on a platter, and cover with foil.

1 hour before:
· Take turkey breast out of refrigerator to come to room temperature.
· When first guest begin to arrive, heat Brie, and place almonds on top.
· Place all appetizers on table; assist guests with beverages.

45 minutes before:
· Take roast out of oven and let it rest.
· Turn oven to 350 degrees and put scalloped potatoes in to warm. You can also heat them

in the microwave, but you don't need to start that process until 30 minutes before dinner.

30 minutes before:
- Turn on coffeemaker; when brewed, put in thermos and prepare the next pot to be turned on right as you serve dinner.
- Prepare serving basket for rolls.
- Carve turkey breast if it is not already spiral cut; garnish with parsley. Cover.
- Replenish beverage table and remind everyone to help themselves.

15 minutes before:
- Have someone carve the meat; cut as thin as possible to allow for maximum servings; garnish platter with parsley. Cover.
- Place rolls in paper bag, sprinkle with water, and place in oven to warm for about 5 minutes.
- Light candles.
- Place salt, pepper, and butter on the table.

Dinner time:
- Place all food on table.
- Turn on second pot of coffee.
- Call you guests to the table.

Dessert:
- Allow guests to finish their meal and then collect the dishes.
- At this point, my husband always pitches in by putting the first load of dishes in the dishwasher or if paper, in the trash bag. If you don't have a helper, leave them until later so you can enjoy the party too. The best of all worlds is to hire a teenager or use a maid service to help cleanup. I have used a service to come in at the time the party starts to follow along behind me and clean up as we progress. By the time the last guest leaves, the kitchen is clean. Now that's a treat!
- Serve the first round of coffee.
- Make the third pot of coffee. Depending on how many takers you have, prepare the coffee beans for a fourth pot.
- Remove the food from the table and put leftovers away.
- Place dessert and dishes on the table. Freshen the coffee thermos.
- Call guests to the table and allow them to serve themselves.

You've done it. Enjoy!

Shopping List

Remember to consider the amounts based on the number of guests you expect. Check your pantry for these staples. Add those you are missing to your weekly shopping list:

____ketchup

____fresh garlic

____cayenne pepper

____Worcestershire sauce

____flour

____soy sauce

____dried parsley

____cinnamon

____sugar

____nutmeg

____cloves

____salt

____dry mustard

____fresh ground pepper

____thyme

____dried red pepper flakes

____coffee

____garlic cloves

____vegetable oil

Here's what you'll need to add to your weekly shopping list:

____rib roast, off the bone

____preroasted turkey breast

____frozen shrimp (shrimp cocktail)

____French bread baguette (Brie)

____rolls

____crackers (Brie and crab appetizer)

____butter or margarine (Brie, spiced nuts, scalloped potatoes, rolls)

____cream cheese (crab appetizer)

____5- to 6-inch wheel of Brie (Brie)

____sour cream (veggie dip, ambrosia)

____milk (scalloped potatoes, coffee)

____bean or rice noodles (cucumber salad, located in the Oriental food section)

____rice vinegar (cucumber salad)

____chili oil (cucumber salad)

____sesame seed oil (cucumber salad)

____sliced almonds (Brie)

____whole almonds, pecans or mixed nuts (spiced nuts)

____canned crab meat, or fresh (crab appetizer)

____dry onion soup mix (veggie dip)

____mandarin oranges (ambrosia)

____pineapple chunks (ambrosia)

____shredded coconut (ambrosia)

____miniature marshmallows (ambrosia)

____cocktail sauce (shrimp, crab appetizer)

____white horseradish (cocktail sauce)

____potatoes (scalloped potatoes)

____parsley (roast, turkey)

____lemon (cocktail sauce)

____onion (crab appetizer, scalloped potatoes)

____raw vegetables (veggie tray)

____cucumbers (salad, veggie tray)

____desserts

____wine

____sparkling cider

____soft drinks

____ice

Shopping List Amounts

You won't need as many appetizers for 12 and 18 guests.

To serve:	12	18	25
rib roast	3 ribs, 6 to 8 lbs	4 ribs, 8 to 10 lbs	5 ribs, 10 to 12 lbs
turkey breast, preroasted	none	none	2 to 3 lbs
frozen or fresh shrimp	1 lb	1 1/2 lbs	1 1/2 lbs
baguette rolls	1 loaf	1 loaf	1 loaf
rolls	1 1/2 dozen	2 dozen	2 1/2 dozen
crackers	1 box	1 box	2 boxes
butter/ margarine	1 lb	1 lb	1 1/2 lbs
cream cheese	none	none	12 ounces
Brie	1	1	1
sour cream	none	none	12 ounces
milk	4 cups	6 cups	8 cups
bean or rice noodles	1 ounce	1 ounce	1 ounce
rice vinegar	1 tablespoon	1 tablespoon	1 tablespoon
chili oil	to taste	to taste	to taste
sesame seed oil	1 teaspoon	1 teaspoon	1 teaspoon
sliced almonds	1/2 cup	1/2 cup	1/2 cup
almonds, pecans, mixed nuts	1 lb	1 lb	1 lb
crab meat, fresh or canned	none	none	6 ounces
onion soup mix	1 package	1 package	1 package
mandarin oranges	1 15-ounce can	1 15-ounce can	2 15-ounce cans
pineapple chunks	1 15-ounce can	1 15-ounce can	2 15-ounce cans
shredded coconut	to fill 15-ounce can once	to fill 15-ounce can once	fill can twice
mini marshmallows	to fill 15-ounce can once	to fill 15-ounce can once	fill can twice
cocktail sauce	2 cups	2 cups	2 cups + 1/2 cup
white horseradish	small bottle	small bottle	small bottle
potatoes	8 medium	12 medium	16 medium
parsley	1 bunch	1 bunch	1 bunch
lemons	1	1	1
onions	1 large	2 large	2 large
carrots	2 large	3 large	4 large
celery	1/2 bunch	1 bunch	1 bunch
mushrooms	1/2 lb	1/2 lb	1/2 lb
cucumbers	6	9	9
jicama	1 large	1 large	2 large
desserts	1 large	2 large	3 large
candles			
other decorations			
wine		1 bottle for every two people, depending on	
sparkling cider		number of drinkers and nondrinkers	

DINNER FOR EIGHT: CHRISTMAS

Spiced Nuts
Ethyl's Cream Cheese Spread and Crackers
Liver Pate and Crackers
Cream of Mushroom Soup
Prime Rib
Yorkshire Pudding
Mashed Potatoes and Gravy
Caesar Salad
Cherry Meringue Pie
Coffee

As with Thanksgiving, our family has its traditions around Christmas. Despite the fact that we celebrate Hanukkah, we have always hosted a dinner and invited friends who do not have a family of their own. We always have standing rib roast—Thanksgiving is still too close to repeat the turkey dinner. Be sure to read this entire plan before beginning preparations.

Planning. We often have about 8 to 10 guests at our holiday table. Although I usually know who is coming at least a week ahead of time, this menu is sufficient to add a few stragglers at the last minute.

You should decide on your menu a week or more before the holiday so you can order the roast from the butcher. Plan to do the majority of the shopping the weekend before, although you'll want to purchase any perishable items the day or two before the dinner. You can serve a hot vegetable in addition to the salad if you like. I have found that with the soup and the Yorkshire Pudding, there is more than enough food. I serve the salad with the meal.

As with the other meals, if you don't need your table, decorate it a day or two before to spread the chores over the week. Be creative with your table decorations. Make a simple centerpiece by placing colorful Christmas ornaments in a crystal bowl flanked by two candles. Or place evergreen boughs down the middle of the table and place candles of any height and color with ornaments in and around the greens.

We usually invite our guests to arrive about an hour or so before dinner and sit down to the table about six. This allows for a fairly relaxed day and an evening that ends at a reasonable hour.

Spiced Nuts

(See page 19 for recipe.)

Variation: Substitute spices above with ½ teaspoon garlic salt, ½ teaspoon curry, and ¼ to ½ teaspoon cayenne pepper, depending on how spicy you like it. Or add 1 teaspoon Worcestershire sauce to the melted butter and follow the rest of the recipe, as above.

Ethyl's Cream Cheese Spread

(courtesy of Linda Cota-Robles)

Our good friend, Linda Cota-Robles, shared her mother's recipe with me. I always keep the ingredients on hand because it is easy to fix on a moment's notice. Mix the following and serve with crackers:

8 ounces cream cheese
2 tablespoons poppy seeds
¾ cup green olives with pimientos, smashed into small pieces

Liver Pate

1 pound chicken livers
1 small onion, chopped
¼ cup butter or margarine
½ teaspoon dried thyme
½ cup sour cream

Melt butter and sauté onions until translucent; transfer to a small bowl. Sauté livers until cooked—they should be slightly pink inside. Add thyme and stir. Put livers and onions through a meat grinder or processor. Add sour cream and mix well. Place in small serving dish, cover, and refrigerate. Serve with crackers.

Tip: Save the wrappers from sticks of butter or margarine, fold, and place in the refrigerator to use later for greasing cookie sheets, muffin tins, or casserole dishes.

Cream of Mushroom Soup

7 cups chicken broth (Make your own or use any readymade variety. I reconstruct my own from chicken-flavored base or bouillon.)
1½ pound mushrooms
5 tablespoons flour
1 teaspoon dry mustard
6 tablespoons butter or margarine
fresh ground pepper
½ cup sherry or dry vermouth
2 cups heavy cream
dried parsley

Wash mushrooms. Remove stems and chop into small pieces. Save the caps and slice right before you add to prevent them from changing color. Heat the broth, add mushroom stems, and simmer for 30 to 35 minutes. When possible, I do this much the day before and when cool, cover, and refrigerate until ready to complete the soup.

About 2 hours before dinner, strain the broth and discard the mushroom pieces. Save the broth in the same pan in which the mushrooms were simmered. Slice the mushroom caps and in a large pot, sauté in the butter until lightly browned. Sprinkle with the flour, dry mustard, and pepper, to taste, and stir until dry ingredients are well mixed with butter and mushrooms. It will look pasty and a little on the lumpy side. Gradually add the broth, stirring continually until it thickens. Set aside until ready to serve.

Immediately before dinner, reheat, add sherry and cream, and stir until hot. I serve about ½ to ¾ cup per person, garnished with a touch of dried parsley. I don't serve larger portions because I want guests to have room for the rest of the meal. I also hope I have a cup or two left over to enjoy the next day!

Variation: If you are really strapped for time, here's a shortcut. It's not as wonderful as homemade but the extra mushrooms and sherry give it an additional zip. If your guest don't see you open the can, they probably won't guess that you didn't slave over a stove for two days!

Use your favorite canned cream of mushroom soup and make as directed. To it, add:

4 large mushrooms per can of soup, sliced, and sautéed in a little butter
2 tablespoons sherry, per can
Garnish with dried parsley.

Prime Rib

3-rib prime rib roast
3 garlic cloves
salt
fresh ground pepper

For 8 to 10 guests, I usually prepare a 3-rib roast. Each rib is between 2 and 2½ pounds and will feed 3 to 4 people. Ask the butcher to prepare the roast by cutting the meat from the bone and tying it back together.
Leave the fat cap in place for extra flavor; the drippings will be used for the Yorkshire Pudding.

Over the years, I have tried many ways to prepare a prime rib and finally have settled on this method. Preheat the oven to 500 degrees. In the meantime, peel the garlic cloves and cut each into about four pieces. With a small paring knife, make a deep cut by pushing the knife into the meat up to the hilt of the knife. Then press your finger into the cut to expand the hole and push in a piece of the garlic. Do the same with the remaining garlic, evenly distributed throughout the roast. Sprinkle the roast with salt and pepper and press into meat.

How long to roast the meat will depend on the size of the prime rib, your oven, and the temperature of the roast when it goes into the oven. In general, I usually go for medium rare, that is, a warm pink center. The ends will be less pink for those who like theirs a little more done and those that like theirs really rare can be appeased by a pinker center. Figure on 18 to 20 minutes per pound. A thermometer placed in the center of the roast (never resting in fat or on a bone) should read 160 degrees right before it is carved.

For a rare roast, figure 15 to 18 minutes and 140 degrees. If you insist on cooking it to death—no pink in the middle—it will take anywhere for 25 to 30 minutes per pound to ruin it! The thermometer will read 170 degrees. (No bias here, folks!)

The roast will need to "rest" for about 30 minutes before it is carved. This allows the juices from the center of the roast to be redistributed to the outer edges, which will have lost its juices in the cooking process. Remember that it will continue to cook even after it is out of the oven. You'll need to take the roast out when it is about 10 degrees below the desired finished temperature of the meat. As soon as I take it out, I always cut into the center to check the real status. If it is already perfect, I break my own rule of letting it rest and carve it immediately, which will stop the cooking process. Slice it as thin as possible and cover the platter with foil to keep it hot. You will lose a great deal of the juice to the platter, but I find this more acceptable than overdone meat!

If your thermometer is accurate and the meat is still below your desired temperature, allow the meat to rest while you complete the rest of your preparations.

Mashed Potatoes and Gravy

9 medium potatoes, peeled and cubed
¼ cup butter or margarine
milk, up to ½ cup (1 or 2 percent)

Figure 1 medium potato per guest and one for the pot. (If you'd like potato pancakes to serve with leftover roast and gravy, add a few extra potatoes.)

Peel potatoes and cut into cubes that are about 2 inches by 2 inches, place in pan, and cover with water. Add a pinch or two of salt. Place lid on pan, bring to a boil (and then uncover or it will boil over), and simmer until a potato will easily fall off a sharp knife inserted into the potatoes. Don't let them get mushy. Pour the potato water into a large measuring cup or bowl and *save for the gravy*. Place the potatoes in a large mixing bowl.

Add margarine and beat with mixer until the big lumps are gone. Add small amounts of milk, about ¼ cup at a time, and mix until you have the creamy texture your family enjoys. I don't add salt and pepper but you can if you wish. Place into serving dish and cover with foil until ready to serve. They can be put into the microwave for a minute right before serving to reheat. You can also use a hand-masher if you prefer.

Gravy

water from potatoes
1½ cups flour
water
salt, to taste
fresh ground pepper, to taste

(See page 7 for additional instructions.)

As soon as the roast comes out of the oven and after you have removed the fat for the Yorkshire Pudding, carefully pour off as much of the remaining grease as possible. Add the water from the potatoes and bring to a boil. If your pan is large enough to cover two burners, turn them both on. Use a fork to scrape the "goodies" off the bottom of the pan...this is where the flavor sits. If you have a good rich flavor and want more gravy, add a little more water to increase the volume. When the liquid comes to a rolling boil, slowly add the gravy thickening while stirring as fast as you can. Continue to add the flour mixture until the gravy is the consistency you like. If you think you need more thickening, just let it boil for a minute or two and see if that gets you to where you want to be. If not, turn the heat off and make a little more thickening, turn the heat back on and get the rolling boil going

again and pick up where you left off. Add salt and pepper, to taste.

If you feel that there aren't enough "brown goodies" on the bottom of the pan to make flavorful gravy, you can add a beef bouillon cube or two to the juices *before* adding the thickening. (Add one at a time to taste.) If you've taken all of the precautions and still get lumps just run the gravy through a sieve as you pour it into the gravy boats at serving time.

Yorkshire Pudding

For each 6 servings use:
1 cup flour
½ teaspoon salt
2 eggs
1 cup milk (Some recipes call for half milk, half cream. I don't notice any significant difference using all 1 or 2 percent milk.)

I always double the recipe as many people like seconds of this treat. But it does not save well as a leftover.

One of the reasons you want to leave the fat cap on the roast is to ensure that you have enough fat in the bottom of the roasting pan to use for the Yorkshire Pudding. My family usually tries to eat healthy throughout the year, but over the holidays, we throw all caution to the wind. (I know that the reason we have January 1 is so we can redirect ourselves back toward the straight and narrow.) If your roast doesn't provide enough fat, you can use bacon fat or butter.

The pudding can be baked in a cake pan or in

muffin tins. I prefer to use the muffin pan, which provides individual servings that are easy to serve. Bring ingredients to room temperature before mixing but plan to prepare in time to refrigerate for at least 2 hours before baking.

Put flour and salt into a large bowl. Gradually stir in the milk and beat with the mixer until smooth. Add one egg at a time. Mix well. Cover and refrigerate. About 10 minutes before the roast is scheduled to come out of the oven, place about 1 tablespoon of hot fat from the roasting pan into each muffin tin and place pan on rack beneath the roast. Fat should become hot, almost to the point of smoking. When the roast is removed, immediately increase temperature to 450 degrees. Pour batter in tin to fill cups halfway. Place pan in oven and bake for about 15 minutes. Reduce heat to 350 degrees and bake for another 10 to 15 minutes until puddings are puffed and lightly browned. Watch closely. Leave in pan until time to transfer to serving dish and place on the table.

Caesar Salad

1½ heads romaine lettuce
1 garlic clove
salt
¼ cup olive oil
2 inches anchovy paste
1 teaspoon balsamic vinegar,
1 teaspoon Worcestershire sauce
1 teaspoon Dijon mustard
1 egg (optional)
1 lemon
½ cup Parmesan cheese
croutons (optional)

Place a few shakes of salt into a large wooden bowl. Peel garlic and smash into the salt, releasing the garlic oil into the bowl. Add about ¼ cup of olive oil and mix with garlic. Let oil sit for at least half hour to blend flavors.

When ready to toss salad, discard the garlic clove, add 2 inches of anchovy paste and "work" with fork until the paste is dissolved in the oil. Add balsamic vinegar, Worcestershire sauce, and Dijon mustard. Mix well. Add egg and mix. I usually discard about half of the yolk to cut down on the cholesterol. (If you are concerned about salmonella from the raw egg, eliminate the egg or use an egg substitute). Add the juice of one lemon and mix. Add lettuce, washed and torn into small pieces, and Parmesan cheese. You may add croutons if you like. Toss and serve.

Cherry Meringue Pie

This festive dessert always gets good reviews! Preheat oven to 275 degrees. Cut a brown paper bag or parchment paper to fit a round pizza or cookie pan. Place your serving plate on bag and draw a circle with a pencil.

For the meringue:
3 egg whites, at room temperature
¼ teaspoon cream of tartar
¾ cup sugar

Separate the egg whites from the yolks. Crack the egg over a separate bowl. There must not be any yolk in the whites or it will not whip correctly. By using a separate bowl, you guard against having to toss the whole thing if you have an accident with a yolk. Save the yolk for another use such as Hollandaise sauce.

Place whites and cream of tartar in mixing bowl and beat with a mixer on high speed until frothy. Very gradually, add the sugar in a small stream and beat until the meringue forms and holds stiff peaks. Pour on to the middle of the brown paper and with a knife or rubber spatula, shape into a resemblance of a pie pan, pushing meringue up at the edges to form sides. *Leave a 1-inch border around the edge of the paper.* The meringue will expand slightly and you want to ensure it will fit on your serving plate.

Bake in the middle of the oven for 1 to 1½ hours. It should be crispy and browned. Turn off oven, open door a notch, and let sit in oven for another hour. Remove from oven and let cool completely before filling.

For the filling:
8 ounces cream cheese, softened
1 teaspoon vanilla
½ cup sugar
1 cup miniature marshmallows
2½ cups whipped topping, such as Cool Whip
21-ounce can cherry pie filling

Mix the first three ingredients with mixer and then stir in marshmallows. Fold in the whipped topping.

To assemble:
I place a doily on the serving platter but you can omit that if you like. Gently lift meringue from paper and place on serving dish. If you have trouble separating the meringue from the paper, place it into a hot oven again for just a minute or two. It should lift off of the paper easily. Spoon the cream mixture into the shell and spread evenly, pushing a little up the sides. Pour berry filling on top. Cover with plastic wrap and refrigerate until serving time.

Variation: You can use any flavor of pie filling for this recipe. Cover half of the pie with blueberries and use cherry on the other to make a great July 4 dessert!)

Tip: When preparing your grocery list, group foods together as they will appear in the food sections in your favorite store, i.e., all items to be found in the dairy case, meat case, canned vegetables, and so forth, and put them on the list according to the path you will take at the store. You'll be less likely to miss items on the list and won't have to go back to the other side of the store because the eggs ended up in the midst of the housekeeping items. You'll be out of the store in half the time.

Timetable

1 week before:

· Order the roast. If they have advance notice, your neighborhood grocery store will usually handle the special request of cutting the meat from the bone and tying it back together.

Several days before:

· If you don't need your dining room table, decorate and set the table.

1 day before:

· Make the Spiced Nuts and store in an airtight container.
· Make Ethyl's Cream Cheese Spread; refrigerate.
· Make liver pate; refrigerate.
· Wash mushrooms. Remove caps and place in bag; refrigerate. Chop stems into small pieces and simmer in broth. When cool, cover and refrigerate.
· Clean and tear lettuce for salad; wrap in wet paper towel, then a kitchen towel; refrigerate.
· Make meringue for the dessert. Store overnight in the oven, uncovered.
· Combine cream cheese, sugar, vanilla, and marshmallows for cream cheese filling for dessert; refrigerate.

Morning or early afternoon on Christmas Day:

· Bring out dessert cream filling mixture and let soften.
· Fold whipped topping into dessert filling and assemble pie; cover with plastic wrap and refrigerate.
· Set table if not done yet.

3½ hours before dinner:

· Peel potatoes, add salt and cover with water; set aside.
· Make gravy thickening.

3 hours before:

· Preheat oven to 500 degrees.
· Prepare roast with garlic and pepper.
· Remove eggs and milk for Yorkshire pudding from the refrigerator and allow to come to room temperature.

2½ hours before:

· Turn oven down to 325 degrees and put meat in the oven.
· Make batter for Yorkshire Pudding and cover with plastic wrap; refrigerate.
· Take time for yourself to relax and get dressed.

2 hours before:

· Finish soup to the point of adding cream and sherry; cover and refrigerate.
· Place salt and garlic in oil for salad.

1½ hours before:
- Boil potatoes and mash. Place in a microwave-safe serving dish or bowl.

1 hour before (guests begin to arrive):
- Check the roast. If the meat is roasting faster than planned, you may need to take it out sooner, let it rest, carve it, and cover with aluminum foil until the rest of the dinner is ready. If this is the case, immediately return the pan with the fat to the oven to keep hot for the Yorkshire Pudding.

- Put Spiced Nuts in serving dish. Serve Ethyl's Cream Cheese Spread and Liver Pate with crackers. Invite guests to serve themselves a drink or appoint a bartender.
- Grind coffee beans for two pots of coffee and place in the filters. Prepare the coffeemaker for the first pot but don't turn on yet.

45 minutes before:
- Take fat from bottom of roasting pan and place in muffin tins; place the tins on rack below the roast to heat.

30 minutes before:
- Turn oven to 450 degrees and immediately take out roast.
- Pour Yorkshire Pudding batter into muffin tins and return to oven.
- Place roast on cutting board or platter to "rest."

- Remove fat from meat juices and make gravy and turn off heat.
- Ask someone to open the wine.
- Make salad dressing and toss salad.

20 minutes before:
- Heat soup and add cream and sherry. Keep on low heat and stir frequently.
- Pour beverages.

15 minutes before:
- Turn oven down to 350 degrees.
- Heat potatoes in microwave.

10 minutes before:
- Carve roast, place on platter, and cover with foil.
- Light candles.

Soup time:
- Remove Yorkshire Pudding from oven and place in serving dish, turn off oven, and set pudding back in oven to keep warm.
- Serve soup and call guests to the table.

Dinner time:
- Clear soup bowls.
- Turn on gravy to reheat; stir well.
- Reheat potatoes for 1 minute in microwave
- Put gravy in serving dish.
- Place food on the table.
- Turn on coffeemaker.
- Pour additional drinks.

· Sit down and enjoy the rest of the meal!

Dessert time:
· After dinner, pour everyone a cup of coffee while the dishes are cleared to the kitchen and the leftovers put away.

· After the chores are completed, allow yourself a moment or two to enjoy your coffee and guests.
· Serve dessert with second cup of coffee.

Tip: When making a meringue or other recipes that require the separation of egg yolks from the white, always prepare each egg individually over a cup, adding the single white to the bowl in which you will do your mixing. This way, if you have an "accident" on the third egg and get a little yolk mixed in with the white, you don't have to throw the whole lot out and start over. In some recipes, it is crucial that no yolk is in with the egg white.

Shopping List

Check your pantry for these staples. Add those you are missing to your shopping list. Don't forget to consider any ingredients you purchased earlier. Likewise, if you have Spiced Nuts in the freezer, you can eliminate those items as well.

_____salt
_____fresh ground pepper
_____Dijon mustard
_____balsamic vinegar
_____Worcestershire sauce
_____flour
_____sugar
_____cinnamon
_____nutmeg
_____ground cloves
_____dry mustard
_____thyme
_____dried parsley
_____vanilla
_____cream of tartar
_____garlic cloves
_____olive oil
_____Parmesan cheese
_____coffee
_____sherry or dry vermouth

Here's what you'll need to add to your weekly shopping list:
_____rib standing rib roast
_____chicken livers
_____ milk (Yorkshire pudding, mashed potatoes), plus milk for drinking
_____butter or margarine (nuts, mushroom soup, mashed potatoes, liver pate)
_____whipping cream (mushroom soup)
_____eggs (Yorkshire pudding, Caesar salad, dessert)
_____sour cream (liver pate)

_____cream cheese (cheese spread, dessert)
_____green olives with pimiento (cheese spread)
_____croutons (salad; optional)
_____crackers (cheese spread, liver pate)
_____cherry pie filling (dessert)
_____poppy seeds (cheese spread)
_____miniature marshmallows (dessert)
_____almonds, pecans, or mixed nuts (spiced nuts)
_____chicken broth or chicken base or bouillon to reconstitute (mushroom soup)
_____beef bouillon (gravy)
_____anchovy paste (Caesar salad)
_____whipped topping (dessert)
_____romaine lettuce (salad)
_____medium-sized mushrooms* (soup)
_____lemon (salad)
_____onion (liver pate)
_____potatoes (mashed potatoes)
_____wine
_____juice or sparkling cider, if desired
_____candles and other decoration needs

* You won't need as many mushrooms if you are using canned cream of mushroom soup; just figure 4 medium mushrooms per can of soup. Don't forget to add the soup to the list. If you are serving another vegetable, don't forget to add to the list.

Shopping List Amounts

For 12 guests, prepare 3 times the recipe of Yorkshire Pudding and 1 1/2 recipes of potatoes. For 16, double the recipes for spiced nuts, liver pate, potatoes, and salad. Prepare 1 1/2 times the recipe for Ethyl's cream cheese spread and soup and 4 times the Yorkshire pudding.

To Serve:	8	12	16
rib roast	3 ribs	4 ribs	5 ribs
chicken livers	1 lb	1 lb	2 lbs
milk	2½ cups	3 3/4 cups	5 cups
butter or margarine	1 cup + 2 tablespoons	1¼ cups	2½ cups
whipping cream	2 cups	2 cups	3 cups
eggs	8	10	12
sour cream	½ cup	½ cup	1 cup
cream cheese	2 8-oz packages	2 8-oz packages	2 8-oz packages
green olives with pimiento	¾ cup	¾ cup	1 cup
crackers	1 box	1 box	2 boxes
cherry pie filling	21-oz can	21-oz can	21-oz can
poppy seeds	2 tablespoons	2 tablespoons	3 tablespoons
miniature marshmallows	1 cup	1 cup	1 cup
almonds, pecans, or mixed nuts	1 lb	1 lb	2 lbs
chicken broth, base, or bouillon	7 cups broth (1 to 5 cubes bouillion)	7 cups broth (1 to 5 cubes bouillion)	10½ cups broth (1 to 8 cubes bouillion)
beef bouillon			
anchovy paste— Find it in a tube near the tuna fish.	small tube	small tube	small tube
whipped topping	2½ cups	2½ cups	2½ cups
romaine lettuce	2 heads	2 heads	3 heads
mushrooms	1½ lbs	1½ lbs	2¼ lbs
lemon	1	1	2
onion	1	1	1
potatoes	9	13	17
sherry—You'll need this even if you use canned soup.	½ cup	½ cup	3/4 cup
candles	2 minimum	4 minimum	4 minimum
other decorations			
camera			
sparkling cider wine	1 bottle for every two people, depending on number of drinkers and nondrinkers		

DINNER FOR EIGHT: NEW YEAR'S EVE

Shrimp Cocktail
Jalapeño Jelly/Cream Cheese
Smoked Salmon and Capers
Beef Tenderloin With Mustard and Bacon Crust
Salad With Feta Cheese, Hazel Nuts, and Raspberry Dressing
Rolls
Basil and Lime Potatoes
Haricots Verts (Green Beans) With Almonds
Mushroom Flan
Chocolate Mousse Tort

We used to have large parties with much food and drink to usher in the new year. We now invite several of our neighbors over for a quiet but festive evening.

Planning. I use a forest green tablecloth, napkins and an assortment of green, ivory, and clear oil candles of various heights and shapes to decorate the table. I tie wide gold ribbon bows to the two tallest candlestick holders placed together in the middle of the table. The ribbon streamers trail around the other candles toward the ends of the table. Metallic gold, ¼-inch ribbons are mounded around the base of the candles to fill in the empty spaces. When the lights are dimmed, the candlelight bounces off of the crystal and metallic ribbon for a sparkling centerpiece!

The entire evening is planned around food and dining in the truest sense of the word. We invite our neighbors to arrive about seven o'clock and start with drinks, appetizers, and much conversation. About an hour or so later, we sit down to the first course of salad. I allow at least a half hour between the salad and the main course. I like to enjoy my company before I have to excuse myself to put the finishing touches on dinner. After dinner, I clear the table, enjoy a cup of coffee, and rest for quite a while before we move on to dessert and another cup of coffee. If we've moved through the evening according to plan, we leave the table with little time to spare before watching the ball come down on Time Square. Some years, we crack open a bottle of champagne to toast in the New Year.

As with other meals, I try to be reasonable with the amount of food choices and the size of the portions. I usually do not serve a vegetable in addition to the salad but have included the Green Beans With Almonds in case you feel the need.

Shrimp Cocktail

1 pound cooked and cleaned frozen shrimp

Defrost under cold running water. Serve over a little crushed ice with Cocktail Sauce. You can buy the sauce or make it yourself.

Cocktail Sauce
2 cups ketchup
2 tablespoons fresh lemon juice
2 teaspoons Worcestershire sauce
white horseradish, to taste

If your horseradish is over a month old, buy a new jar; it loses its zip very quickly. Combine the first three ingredients, then add the horseradish. Start by adding 1 tablespoon, mix well, and continue adding small amounts until the sauce has the desired punch.

Jalapeño Jelly Over Cream Cheese

8 ounces jalapeño jelly
8-ounce package cream cheese
assorted crackers

Serve jelly over a block of cream cheese with crackers.

Jalapeño Jelly

I enjoy making this on a Sunday afternoon in the fall. It makes a great holiday or hostess gift. Of course, you can always purchase a jar of readymade jelly.

3 cups green bell pepper, seeded and cut into small pieces (about 1 medium pepper per cup)
1 cup jalapeño peppers, seeded and cut into small pieces (about 1 medium jalapeño per ¼ cup—increase the amount of jalapeños if you like a hotter taste)
3 cups white or apple cider vinegar
12 cups of sugar
2 packages of liquid pectin (I buy a brand that has two pouches per package; I have not had success using any of the powdered gelatins)
green food coloring

How spicy you like the jelly will dictate if you add any of the jalapeño seeds and if so, how many. When I first made this jelly, the recipe I used called for a 1-to-6 ratio of jalapeño to bell peppers. I have completely changed those proportions. I gradually started to leave a few of the jalapeño seeds in with the peppers. Now I don't remove any of the seeds for a spicy but not burning flavor.

In a blender, add small amounts of the peppers with some of the vinegar and puree. Do the same with all the rest of the peppers. Combine the pureed peppers, any remaining vinegar and sugar in a very large pan and bring to a boil. (Watch this very closely! If it boils over, you'll have a mess!) When you can't stir down the boil anymore, remove it from the heat and let it sit for about 5 minutes. Skim. Add the gelatin and enough food coloring to make it a bright green. Stir until mixed thoroughly.

Pour into sterilized jars. This amount will fill about 20 8-ounce jars. Leave at least a ½ inch of space at the top. When cooled and jelled, melt paraffin in an old saucepan and pour about ¼ inch on the top of each jar. Put on lids and tighten securely. Jelly will store for months.

Smoked Salmon and Capers

6 ounces smoked salmon
½ cup capers
crackers

Buy a small package of smoked salmon or obtain from the deli. Cut into cracker-size pieces, arrange on a small serving dish, and serve with ½ cup capers. I put the capers in a small custard cup and place them on the salmon dish. Some folks like to serve a little cream cheese with this also; it can go on the same serving dish.

Salad With Feta Cheese, Hazelnuts, and Raspberry Dressing

mixed salad greens, 1 cup per person
4 medium-sized mushrooms
1 cup crumbled feta cheese
¾ cup toasted, chopped hazelnuts
½ cup Raspberry Dressing (more, if desired)

Place the hazelnuts in a pie or cake pan and place in a preheated, 350-degree oven until toasted lightly. Watch carefully; they will take no longer than about 5 to 7 minutes. Remove from oven and immediately place in a kitchen towel and rub together briskly to remove as many of the skins as possible. Be careful not to burn yourself when handling them. Chop, leaving in fairly large pieces.

Wash and drain salad greens; wash and slice mushrooms. Mix together and toss with dressing. Distribute evenly between salad plates. Equally divide feta cheese and nuts between the servings.

You may also serve with dinner rolls, if desired. (See page 8.)

Variation: Add several slices of ripe, peeled pears to each salad for a delicious change.

Raspberry Dressing

1/3 cup raspberry vinegar
2 tablespoon water
¾ cup vegetable oil
2 tablespoon Dijon mustard
dash of garlic powder
¼ teaspoon thyme

Combine together in a jar with a lid and shake to mix.

Beef Tenderloin With Mustard and Bacon Crust

(compliments of Jackie Rindin)

4 to 5 pounds beef tenderloin
6 slices bacon, chopped into small pieces
2 garlic cloves, minced
6 tablespoons butter, brought to room temperature
3 tablespoons Dijon mustard
½ teaspoon thyme
fresh ground pepper, to taste (about three good turns of the pepper mill)

I have changed Jackie's recipe ever so slightly by altering the amounts and adding the thyme.

Put the bacon through a meat grinder and then mix with all of the other ingredients. If you don't have a grinder, cut bacon into very small pieces and mash together with a fork. Pat over the meat, place on a rack in a roasting pan. Preheat the oven to 450 degrees and roast for about 30 minutes. Turn off the oven and without opening the oven, let it sit for another half hour. I don't know how it does this, but it comes out to a perfect medium-rare every single time! Don't forget to let it sit for about 10 minutes before carving to let the juices settle. Slice thinly and garnish platter with parsley.

Basil and Lime Potatoes

1 small potato per person, peeled and cut into 1-inch slices
1 tablespoon dried or ¼ cup fresh basil, finely chopped
1 tablespoon lime zest
2 teaspoons fresh lime juice
2 tablespoons olive oil

Cover potatoes with water and parboil until they begin to soften. Be careful not to overcook as they will turn to mush further on in the process. Place in a large Ziploc plastic bag with the oil and mix until oil is evenly distributed. Place them in a small roasting pan (cake pan will do) and place them in the oven when you put the roast in. When the roast is done, pull the potatoes also. Sprinkle with the lime juice, zest and basil and mix thoroughly. Cover with foil and slip back into the turned off oven until ready to serve.

Use a small grater to remove the lime zest. You can substitute orange for the lime to change the recipe another time.

Haricots Verts (Green Beans) and Almonds

haricots verts *(small tender green beans), about 8 per person*
½ cup almond slivers
2 tablespoons butter or margarine

Wash beans and steam in double boiler until tender but crisp. (If you have a microwave, this step can be done earlier in the day.) Melt butter in small skillet, add almonds, and stir until toasted lightly. Toss the beans and almonds together. Place in serving dish, lengthwise. Can be heated for a minute in the microwave right before serving so they are piping hot.

Mushroom Flan

3 tablespoon butter or margarine
¾ pounds mushrooms, washed and sliced very thin
6 eggs
2¼ cups heavy cream
dash nutmeg
2 tablespoons chopped chives
½ cup fresh basil, finely chopped
fresh ground pepper

Sauce

1¼ cup heavy cream
3 tablespoons lemon juice
2 cups steamed spinach leaves with stems removed, finely chopped

Preheat oven to 350 degrees. Butter 8 ¾-cup ramekins.

Melt butter in skillet and sauté mushrooms until all of the liquid is evaporated and mushrooms are very dry. In a large bowl, whisk together eggs, cream, nutmeg, chives, basil, and a little fresh ground pepper. Add the mushrooms. Grease the ramekins with butter and place about ½ cup in each. Set ramekins in a pan, place in oven, and add water to halfway up the sides of the dishes. Cover pan with foil. Bake for about 45 to 50 minutes until flan is firm to the touch.

When you remove from the oven, you can leave in the pan with the water. It will keep them warm while rest of meal is being prepared.

For the sauce, wash and cut the spinach into thin strips. Blanche in boiling water for 30 second, pour into sieve, and immediately plunge into ice cold water to stop the cooking process. Drain, pressing any liquid from the spinach, and place on paper towel and pat dry. In a small saucepan, bring cream to a simmer—do not boil. Add spinach and simmer until hot. Add lemon juice and remove from the heat. Lemon juice will thicken cream.

Run a knife around the edge of each ramekin, turn over and release flan onto plate. Pour spoonful of sauce over each flan. Serve immediately.

Chocolate Mousse Torte

Over the years, I have combined and tweaked a number of recipes to come up with this favorite. The torte is easy to make. Sometimes I simply serve it with a dollop of whipped cream. By changing the recipe slightly, you can come up with a number of different desserts. This recipe can be prepared on the day it is served but needs to be refrigerated for a minimum of 8 hours. The cake can be made even three days before it is served, covered, and refrigerated.

Cake

1 cup butter or margarine
1½ cups semisweet chocolate chips
¾ cups sugar
5 large eggs, lightly beaten
½ cup almonds, ground

Preheat oven to 325 degrees. Butter a 9-inch-diameter springform pan (2½-inch sides). Line the bottom with parchment, butter it, and dust the pan with flour. Melt the butter and chocolate in a heavy large saucepan over low heat until melted. Stir constantly and keep the heat low so the bottom doesn't burn. Remove from the heat and whisk in the sugar, eggs, and almonds. Pour the batter into the pan and bake about 35 to 40 minutes or until a toothpick inserted into the center comes out clean. The top will have cracks and the torte will be very moist. Cool completely on a cake rack.

Release the sides of the pan and carefully place the cake onto a clean surface. I leave the cake on the bottom of the pan rather than try to take it off and keep it from breaking. Cut off a ½ inch of the cake from around the edge with a sharp knife. Wash and dry the cake pan sides and spray with vegetable oil. Reattach the sides. There will be a space around the cake that will soon be filled with mousse. Cover and refrigerate until ready to frost.

Mousse

2 cups cream
3 teaspoons unflavored gelatin
¼ cup water
16 ounces imported white chocolate, chopped
6 tablespoon sour cream
2 cups whipping cream
6 ounces white chocolate
cocoa powder, to dust the top
fresh strawberries or raspberries, for decoration (optional)

Sprinkle gelatin over the water in a small bowl and let stand for about 10 minutes until softened.

Heat cream over low heat until hot but not boiling. Add the gelatin mixture and stir until dissolved. Stir in the white chocolate and whisk over low heat until melted and smooth. Whisk in the sour cream. Put in large bowl and refrigerate until cool and thickened but not set. Whisk occasionally. If it starts to set, simply whisk until it is smooth again. This takes about 2 hours.

Beat the whipping cream until it holds stiff peaks. (It will whip faster if you chill the bowl and the beaters in the freezer.) Be sure not to over beat or you'll end up with butter! Fold whipped cream into the white chocolate mixture. Pour over the cake, making sure that it covers the sides as well as the top. Refrigerate overnight.

Run a knife around the edges of the cake pan and release and remove the sides. Place a doily on the serving dish and place the cake on the dish. I have not been successful in making wonderful chocolate shavings like you see in the pictures. I have the best success putting the piece of chocolate in the microwave for about 15 seconds—don't let it melt—then use a vegetable peeler to shave off thin curls. Press the shavings onto the sides and sprinkle the rest on the top. Put a tablespoon of cocoa in a fine sieve and dust the top of the cake lightly. Garnish with raspberries or strawberries, if desired, right before serving.

Be creative and this basic recipe will never grow old.

Variation: Forget making the mousse and serve the cake by itself with a spoonful of whipped cream. Add a few raspberries or strawberries if you like.

Variation: Serve the cake (no mousse) with a scoop of your favorite ice cream and a drizzle of chocolate sauce.

Variation: Use ground hazelnuts or pecans in the cake instead of almonds. Fold in ¼ cup of hazelnut liqueur to the mousse mixture at the same time you add the sour cream.

Variation: Substitute mint chocolate chips for the semisweet chocolate in the cake. When making the mousse, fold in a few tablespoons of crème de menthe liqueur to the white chocolate mixture when adding the sour cream. Add a few drops of green food coloring to the mousse—a great St. Patrick's day dessert!

Variation: Add 1 teaspoon orange zest along with the sugar, eggs, and almonds when making the cake. When making the mousse, use ¼ cup of lemon juice instead of water when softening the gelatin. (The lemon juice adds just a touch of tang to the mousse). Fold in ¼ cup orange flavored liqueur when adding the sour cream to the mousse. Add food coloring to make the mousse a light orange.

Tip: When whipping cream, always chill the bowl and beaters in the freezer before hand. The cream will whip much faster. An hour in the freezer is good but anytime is better than none at all.

Timetable

1 week before dinner:
· Order roast.
· Make jalapeño jelly. (This can be done anytime during the previous year.)

3 days before:
· If you have the time, make the cake for the chocolate torte and refrigerate; otherwise, move this chore to the day before the party.

1 day before:
· If possible, make the table decoration and set the table.
· If serving champagne, place in refrigerator to cool.
· Make cocktail sauce for the shrimp.
· Make the salad dressing and refrigerate.
· Combine bacon, garlic, butter, Dijon mustard, thyme, and pepper for the meat. Cover and refrigerate.
· Make the mousse and assemble the dessert including the chocolate shavings and cocoa. *If garnishing with raspberries or strawberries, don't put on until right before serving time as the juice tends to spread on the mousse.*

In the morning the day of the dinner:
· Put finishing touches on the table; don't forget the salt and pepper.
· Optional for dessert: pick about 10

wonderful raspberries or strawberries, wash, dry, and set aside in the refrigerator.
· Defrost shrimp under running water, drain, cover, and refrigerate
· Toast hazelnut for salad, chop and set aside
· Peel potatoes and parboil. *Do not over cook!* Drain and place in Ziploc bag.
· While potatoes are boiling, wash and chop the basil for the potatoes and the flan
· Grate the zest off the lime and squeeze juice from lime.
· If having *haricots verts*, wash and clip ends and steam; refrigerate. If no microwave, wait until 30 minutes before dinner to steam.
· Wash spinach, blanche, chop, and refrigerate.
· Wash mushrooms for flan, slice and sauté; refrigerate
· Wash and drain salad greens and mushrooms; refrigerate.
· If you do not have two ovens, prepare the flan, bake and refrigerate when cool; you can reheat in the microwave or place in the oven at 350 degrees after you have removed the roast from the oven, while you put the finishing touches on the rest of the meal.

3½ hours before:
· Take an hour for yourself to rest and get dressed.

2½ hours before (30 minutes before guests begin to arrive):

- Set up the bar if serving mixed drinks.
- Grind the coffee beans for two pots and prepare coffeemaker for the first one but do not turn on yet.
- Place crackers in a basket; place all appetizers on their respective serving dishes and refrigerate.
- Toast almonds for beans.

2 hours before:
- Guests arrive; make them comfortable and serve drinks and appetizers

1 hour and 40 minutes before main course:
- Preheat oven to 450 degrees.
- Place potatoes in bottom of a roasting pan.
- Pat the bacon and mustard "crust" on the roast and place on rack in roasting pan

1½ hours before main course:
- Toss mushrooms and mixed greens with dressing and assemble salads; place on table.
- If you have a second oven, preheat to 350 degrees to bake flan.

1¼ hours before:
- Place rolls in a paper bag, sprinkle with water, and place in other oven for 5 minutes. If you only have one oven, start 5 minutes earlier and place rolls in the meat oven for 5 minutes and remove, *then* put in the meat and potatoes.
- Place potato pan on the rack beneath the meat.

- Put meat in the oven and set timer for 30 minutes
- Place flan in second oven and set timer for 45 minutes
- Pour beverages.
- Place butter on table.

1 hour and 10 minutes before:
- Take rolls out of oven, place in basket, and put on table.
- Light candles.

1 hour before:
- Sit down to first course.
- *Make sure you listen for the oven timer to go off in 15 minutes!*

45 minutes before:
- Excuse yourself for a moment and turn oven off. *Do not open the oven door!* Let meat sit for another 30 minutes.

30 minutes before:
- Excuse yourself and allow your guests to relax while you clear the table and prepare the main course.
- If baking flan, take out of oven and let sit in water to stay warm.
- If no microwave, steam the *haricots verts*; remove pan from heat and let sit over the water in the double boiler until time to assemble; if beans are already steamed, reheat in microwave just until warm.

15 minutes before:
- Take meat out of oven and let it rest
- If you baked the flan earlier in the day, immediately turn oven to 350 degrees and put flan ramekins in the oven to reheat.
- Make sauce for flan.
- Toss *haricots verts* with almonds and place in serving dish.
- Place potatoes in serving dish.
- Assemble flan; run knife around edge and turn over on dinner plate. Spoon small amount of sauce onto each flan.

5 minutes before:
- Carve meat and place on platter; garnish with parsley and cover with aluminum foil. (You may want to ask for help carving while you prepare the rest of the meal.)
- When this is finished, you are ready to place all dishes on the table.
- Turn on coffeemaker.

- Replenish beverages.
- Serve dinner.

After dinner:
- Clear dishes, serve coffee, and place remainder in a carafe.
- Make second pot of coffee.

Dessert:
- We like to sit for quite a while and let dinner settle before dessert.
- Serve dessert with another cup of coffee, wine or after dinner drink.

10 minutes before midnight:
- Uncork champagne.
- At midnight, make a toast to your good friends, the blessings you have all enjoyed in the past year, and wishes for more of the same in the year to come!

Shopping List

If you are serving more than eight people, you will need to adjust the grocer list accordingly. Check your pantry for these staples. Add those you are missing to your weekly shopping list.

____fresh ground pepper
____cocoa
____Dijon mustard
____garlic powder
____garlic cloves
____ketchup
____nutmeg
____thyme
____green food coloring
____olive oil
____vegetable oil
____Worcestershire sauce
____coffee

Here's what you'll need to add to your weekly shopping list:
____whole beef tenderloin
____bacon (roast)
____small jar white horseradish (cocktail sauce)
____sour cream (dessert)
____feta cheese (salad)
____butter or margarine (meat, green beans, flan, dessert, rolls)
____cream cheese (jalapeño jelly and crackers, salmon)
____eggs (flan, dessert)
____heavy cream (flan, dessert, coffee)
____crackers (appetizers)
____dinner rolls, optional
____paraffin (jelly)
____jars (jelly)
____semisweet chocolate chips (dessert)

____imported white chocolate (dessert; a large block is preferable for making the shavings)
____hazel nuts (salad)
____almond slivers (green beans, dessert)
____liquid pectin (jelly)
____sugar (jelly, dessert)
____unflavored gelatin (dessert)
____white or cider vinegar (jelly)
____raspberry vinegar (salad dressing; may need to go to a specialty cooking store)
____capers (salmon appetizer)
____smoked salmon (appetizer)
____frozen shrimp (appetizer)
____small green beans, or *haricots verts* (vegetable, optional)
____potatoes (vegetable)
____lemons (cocktail sauce, flan)
____fresh mushrooms (salad, flan)
____green bell peppers (jelly)
____jalapeño peppers (jelly)
____mixed salad greens
____lime with healthy-looking skin (potatoes)
____fresh basil (potatoes, flan)
____fresh chopped chives
____fresh spinach leaves, no stems (flan)
____raspberries or strawberries (dessert; optional)
____wine
____champagne
____soft drinks

Shopping List Amounts

For 12 guests, you'll need to prepare 1 1/2 times the recipes for the salad, rolls, potatoes, *haricots verts*, and flan; for 16, double the recipes.

To serve:	8	12	16
beef tenderloin	4 to 5 lbs	4 to 5 lbs	5 to 6 lbs
bacon	6 slices	6 slices	6 slices
white horseradish	small jar	small jar	small jar
sour cream	6 tablespoons	6 tablespoons	6 tablespoons
feta cheese	3 ounces	4½ ounces	6 ounces
butter/margarine	1½ lb	1 3/4 lbs	2 lbs
cream cheese	12 ounces	16 ounces	16 ounces
eggs	11	14	17
heavy cream	6½ cups	8½ cups	12 cups
sugar	13 cups	13 cups	13 cups
unflavored gelatin	3 teaspoons	3 teaspoons	3 teaspoons
white or cider vinegar	3 cups	3 cups	3 cups
raspberry vinegar	1/3 cup	1/3 cup	1/3 cup
capers	6- or 7-ounce jar	6- or 7-ounce jar	6- or 7-ounce jar
smoked salmon	6 ounces	9 ounces	12 ounces
shrimp	1 lb	1 lb	1½ lbs
small green beans	64	96	128
potatoes	8	12	16
lemons	3	4	5
mushrooms	3/4 lb + 4	1 lb + 6	1½ lb + 8
green bell peppers	3 (3 cups)	3 (3 cups)	3 (3 cups)
jalapeno peppers	4 medium (1 cup)	4 medium (1 cup)	4 medium (1 cup)
mixed salad greens	8 cups	12 cups	16 cups
limes	1 to 2	3 to 4	5 to 6
fresh basil	3/4 cup	1 cup	1½ cups
fresh chives	2 tablespoons	3 tablespoons	4 tablespoons
fresh spinach	2 cups	3 cups	4 cups
raspberries	small container	small container	small container
crackers	1 box	1 box	1 box
dinner rolls	1 dozen	1½ dozen	2 dozen
semi-sweet chocolate chips	10-ounce bag	10-ounce bag	10-ounce bag
imported white chocolate	22 ounces	22 ounces	22 ounces
hazel nuts	3/4 cup	1 cup	1½ cups
almond slivers	1 cup	1 1/4 cups	1½ cups
jelly jars	20 to 24	20 to 24	20 to 24
liquid pectin	2 packages	2 packages	2 packages
candles	2 (minimum)	4 (minimum)	4 (minimum)
sparkling cider	1 bottle for every two people, depending on		
wine	number of drinkers and nondrinkers		

SPECIAL DINNER FOR TWO: VALENTINE'S DAY

Duck Pate and Crackers
Rack of Lamb
Twice-Baked Potatoes
Garden Salad With Pine Nuts and Bleu Cheese
Red Wine
Coffee
Valentine Cookies or Cherry Meringue Pie

A special dinner for two doesn't have to wait until February 14, nor does it need to be complicated. Since Valentine's Day often falls during the week, many women (or men) don't have all day to spend in the kitchen. This is a time when spending a little time setting the mood will make the difference between a "throw together" dinner in front of the TV and memorable evening. Keep the menu easy but prepare something that isn't on your list of usual weeknight dinner for the family. Take time to have a cocktail or glass of wine before dinner to help set the mood and acknowledge that this night is different. This simple menu is easy and elegant.

Planning. If you have children who need dinner also, make the evening special for them as well. Treat them to a "picnic" in front of the TV with their favorite fast food or pizza. Make Valentine cookies with them the weekend before and give each child his or her own specially decorated cookie for dessert. Or surprise them with a Valentine's Day "sweet treat" from your favorite candy store.

If it will be a real push to serve dinner at a reasonable time, set the dining room table for two the evening before. A very simple setting, with tablecloth and linen napkins, your good china, and candles will let your honey know this is no ordinary dinner.

Try to do as much ahead of time as possible. Buy pate at your favorite gourmet shop the weekend before. Serve baked potatoes for the family the night before and cook two extra. After dinner, make the potatoes, cover with plastic wrap and refrigerate. Purchase European mix salad at the store that only needs to be washed. Make your favorite salad dressing the weekend before or purchase a bottled dressing at the store. Depending on the time you have that day, you can make an exotic dessert or simply serve cookies that have been decorated the weekend before. If cookie or pie baking adds too much stress, stop by the bakery and pick up a yummy treat.

Pate With Crackers

Purchase a small slab of duck or liver pate at your favorite gourmet market. About 30 minutes before serving, remove from the refrigerator, place on a special dish, and allow to soften. Serve with crackers and your favorite cocktail or beverage.

Rack of Lamb

8-rib rack of lamb
1 piece white bread
2 garlic cloves
1 tablespoon olive oil
1 tablespoon fresh parsley, chopped
several sprigs fresh rosemary
½ teaspoon thyme
2 tablespoons Dijon mustard
fresh ground pepper, to taste

Preheat oven to 375 degrees. Rinse the lamb under water and pat dry. Cut off excess fat. Cover the rib bones with aluminum foil to prevent burning. Rub entire meat surface with garlic put through a press. Spread the meat surfaces with the mustard and place the rack on a few sprigs of rosemary in a roast pan, bone side down. Place more rosemary on top of the rack of lamb. Roast for 25 minutes.

In the meantime, tear the bread into tiny pieces (or place large pieces in blender. Use a few short "hits" of the button to make fine crumbs.) Place in a small bowl with the second garlic clove (which has been put through a press), olive oil, thyme, parsley, and a few turns of fresh ground pepper. Mix well together.

Remove lamb from oven after 25 minutes. Remove rosemary from top of rack and set aside, sprinkle with the bread crumb mixture to cover all visible surfaces and press into meat; return rosemary to top of meat. Return to oven and roast for another 15 minutes for rare, 20 minutes for medium-rare, and 25 minutes for well done. Remove from oven and let stand for about 10 minutes before serving. Remove foil from the bones. Slice between the bones and arrange 4 ribs on each plate. Garnish with a fresh sprig of rosemary.

Twice-Baked Potatoes

2 potatoes
1 tablespoon butter or margarine
Small amount milk
1 tablespoon fresh minced chives
4 tablespoon grated cheddar cheese
Salt and fresh ground pepper to taste

Scrub potatoes, pierce in several places with a knife and bake at 350 degrees for 1 hour or until done (fork inserted in center meets no resistance). Cool, so they can be handled and cut in half length-wise. Remove the "innards" from the potatoes and mash with butter, chives and salt and pepper. Add a little milk to make the consistency of mashed potatoes. Divide the mixture in quarters and "stuff" the jackets; sprinkle each with a tablespoon of cheese. If not going to use immediately, cover with plastic wrap and refrigerate. Place in 350-degree oven for about 30 minutes until hot or heat in microwave for about 4 minutes until hot.

Garden Salad With Pine Nuts and Bleu Cheese

3 cups washed European salad mix
2 mushrooms, cleaned and sliced
1 small tomato, chopped
½ stalk celery, sliced
2 tablespoons toasted pine nuts
2 tablespoons crumbled bleu cheese
salad dressing

Place pine nuts in a pie pan and put in oven for about 3 to 5 minutes at 350 to 375 degrees.

Watch closely! One they start to brown, they go fast! (You can also toast them in a toaster oven. These can be done several days ahead of time. Store in an airtight container for a few days or place in a plastic bag and freeze.) Set aside.

Shortly before serving time, divide the first 4 ingredients into two salad bowls. Garnish with nuts and cheese. Serve with your favorite dressing.

Valentine Cookies

This recipe, also known as Aunt Myrnie's Cut-Out Cookies, is great for any holiday cutout cookie (Valentine, Christmas or Hanukkah) and is the one we have used in our family ever since I can remember. You can substitute margarine for butter, but I think the flavor is better with butter.

1 cup butter, room temperature
1 cup sugar
2 eggs
3 tablespoons milk
4 cups flour
½ teaspoon baking soda

Cream together the butter and sugar; add eggs, and mix well. Add milk. Sift together flour and baking soda. Add gradually to the butter mixture. It will come together in a firm ball.

Preheat oven to 350 degrees

Roll out dough onto a floured surface to 1/8-inch thickness. Cut out cookies in shape of a heart. Reform the leftover dough into another ball and roll out again but only handle enough to form the ball; kneading it too much will make the cookies tough, not flaky. Place on greased cookie sheet and bake until just lightly brown around the edges. Remove baked cookies to a rack or brown paper sack to cool. Frost.

Frosting

I think prepared frosting is just fine, but if you want to make it from scratch you can do the following:

2 cups powdered sugar
½ cup margarine
1 teaspoon vanilla
milk
red and white food coloring
red sprinkles

Place powdered sugar in a bowl and mix with margarine. Add vanilla; then add milk, 1 teaspoon at a time, until it is a good spreading consistency. Add food coloring to desired color. You can divide it in two; color one a nice shade of pink and leave the other one white. Use red sprinkles to decorate. Place a small amount of frosting in the bottom corner of a small plastic Ziploc bag. Cut a tiny hole in the corner and force the frosting through the hole, writing your Valentine's name on a cookie.

Let cookies dry for a few hours and store in an airtight container, separating layers with waxed paper.

Cherry Meringue Pie

Follow the recipe on page 34 but make the meringue in the shape of a heart. I cut a pattern and draw around it on the paper that will be placed on the cookie sheet. Make sure it will fit your serving dish.

Tip: When using a tablecloth and napkins that have been crammed into a drawer or closet for a while, simply wet one of the napkins and place with the other linens in the dryer for about 5 minutes. Remove and immediately place onto the table and smooth. Smooth and fold napkins. You won't need to pull out the iron.

Timetable

The weekend before Valentine's Day:
- Make and frost cookies.
- Toast pine nuts and store in airtight container.
- Shop for nonperishables.

1 day before:
- Shop for perishables.
- Bake potatoes and prepare.
- Set table.
- Chill wine, if needed.
- Prepare salad dressing if not using readymade dressing.
- Make cherry meringue pie, cover with plastic wrap, and refrigerate. You can wait to put the cherries on the pie until serving time.

Valentine's Day:
- If you have children to feed, start about 2½ hours before you want to sit down to eat. Put a pizza or fast food on the table and let them eat while you begin your preparations.

2 hours before:
- Take pate and potatoes out of refrigerator to warm to room temperature.
- Make salads and place in refrigerator.
- Put finishing touches on the table.
- Prepare coffeemaker but don't turn on.
- Prepare lamb for oven.

- Place crackers in basket.

1 hour and 20 minutes before:
- Preheat oven to 375 degrees.
- Get the kids ready for bed.

1 hour before:
- Put lamb in oven.
- Fix your Valentine's favorite cocktail and ask him or her to join you for an appetizer.
- Serve the kids their Valentine cookies for dessert.

40 minutes before:
- Put potatoes in oven along side of lamb.

35 minutes before:
- Take lamb out and put on crumbs.
- Return lamb to oven
- If you have young children, try to get them in bed now—or situated in front of the TV or with a good book

15 minutes before:
- Take lamb out and let rest.
- Fill water glasses and place on table.
- Pour wine.
- Turn on coffee.
- Place salads and dressing on table.
- Light candles on table.

Dinner time:
- Carve lamb and place on plates, garnish with rosemary; place potatoes on plates and serve.
- Sit down with your honey and enjoy!

Dessert time:
- Don't rush through dinner. When you have finished your meal, sit for a while and enjoy a little more wine or just savor the moment. Then clear the dishes, put cherries on pie, and pour a cup of coffee. Serve dessert.

Tips: Make an inexpensive centerpiece for your kitchen table with artichokes and lemons. Purchase about four artichokes and place in an attractive bowl or basket. Place some lemons in the bowl under and around the artichokes. The artichokes will eventually dry out to a dusky green with purple accents. Use the lemons as needed in your everyday cooking and simply replace as necessary.

Tip: A tip from my husband: Put lemon and orange rinds into the garbage disposal to freshen it.

Shopping List

Check your pantry for these staples. Add those you are missing to your weekly shopping list.

____bread

____milk

____garlic cloves

____cream of tartar

____salt

____pepper

____coffee

____flour

____sugar

____vanilla

____baking soda

____dried thyme

____Dijon mustard

____red and white food coloring

____olive oil

Here's what you'll need to add to your weekly shopping list:

____pate (appetizer)

____rack of lamb

____margarine (potatoes, frosting)

____butter (cookies)

____eggs (meringue pie,* cookies)

____cream cheese (meringue pie)*

____Cool Whip or other whipped topping (meringue pie)*

____grated cheddar cheese (potatoes)

____crumbled bleu cheese (salad)

____pine nuts (salad)

____crackers (pate)

____salad dressing (salad)

____cherry pie filling (meringue pie)*

____miniature marshmallows (meringue pie)*

____powdered sugar (frosting)

____red sprinkles (cookies)

____fresh parsley (lamb)

____fresh rosemary (lamb)

____fresh chives (potatoes)

____potatoes for baking

____European salad mix

____fresh mushrooms (salad)

____celery (salad)

____tomato (salad)

____wine

*   If making the cookies for dessert for both you and the children, eliminate the ingredients for the Cherry Meringue Pie.

DINNER FOR TWENTY: PASSOVER

Gefilte Fish
Brisket and Gravy
Mashed Potatoes
Charoses
Steamed Broccoli
Flourless Chocolate Cake With Strawberries
Kosher Wine
Sparkling Cider
Coffee

This is my favorite religious holiday. Each year we gather with family and friends (many of whom are not Jewish) to celebrate our heritage. It is a festive evening filled with tradition, sentiment, and laughter. We generally have a minimum of 20 guests and occasionally have had as many as 32. Space is the only limiting factor. You could use the main menu for any large gathering. Our family does not keep a Kosher home but for Passover, we often attempt to keep the tradition and prepare the food in a Kosher-style fashion. I have given alternative recipes from the ones we traditionally use for those who prefer to have a kosher-style meal. Those of you who keep a Kosher home will know the rules for a Kashrut meal.

Kashrut, or kosher, is a complete written code of religious dietary laws that govern every act of eating. While the principles include rules for how animals are slaughtered and prepared, probably most notable are limitations in what foods can be eaten singly or in combination. Jews who "keep kosher" do not mix meat and dairy products at the same meal. In addition, they only eat meat from animals with a cloven foot and a parted hoof that chew their cud. This eliminates pork, horse, rabbit, and whale. They eat only fish that have fins and scales, which eliminates shellfish. Certain foods, such as eggs, fish, and vegetables, are considered "pareve," or neutral, and can be eaten with meat or dairy meals.

Many packaged foods are now marked with a symbol to show that they have been approved by a Jewish organization as kosher. Kosher meat is usually found in a kosher butcher shop, but you may find some kosher meat—usually chicken—in the freezer section of some grocery stores.

Planning: This dinner takes a great deal of preparation and time. Only your space and the number of dishes, glasses and silverware will limit the number of guests. In a real pinch, you can always rent what you need for 20, including linens. For the service, you will need the following:

- Seder plate (You may use a regular platter or the special Seder plate, which has places marked for the appropriate traditional food. We use at least two for 20 guests, one at each end of the table.)
- Shabbat candlestick holders
- Elijah's wine goblet (This can be a special goblet used only for Passover or a regular wine glass.)
- Small dishes with salt water placed so that everyone can reach
- Pillow to be placed on the leader's chair (symbolizes resting or reclining)
- Large bowl, pitcher filled with water, towel
- Afikomen cover or towel in which to wrap the dessert or Matzoh
- Matzoh
- Haggadah (prayer book) for all participants and pens for each end of the table

- Kipah for all men
- Place cards (this allows you to strategically place non-Jews next to those who can help them through the service.)
- Camera

My kitchen and dining room tables, with all the leaf extensions, will seat 20 guests. I have occasionally added a card table and our patio table to accommodate more guests. Before I acquired enough tablecloths and napkins for this crowd, I rented. We also borrowed chairs from neighbors or asked friends to bring folding chairs.

I use three sets of candlestick holders down the center of the table. Small bouquets of fresh flowers in short vases add to the festivity of the table and don't take up a great deal of space and are low enough for guests to see over.

Through the years, I have learned that the easiest way to set the table is to first develop the seating plan ahead of time and make the place cards. After putting on the tablecloths, arrange the place cards appropriately. At each setting, place a salad plate on top of a dinner plate, followed by a Haggadah. Place a kipah on top of the settings for the gentlemen. The evening begins with the Passover service and you will use the salad plate for the ceremonial foods. When you break for the meal, remove the dessert plate and the dinner plate will already be in place.

Place a knife, fork, and spoon at each place. Our experience is that not all guests enjoy gefilte fish, so we give the soupspoon when we serve the fish. We also reserve the dessert forks and bring them out with the dessert.

Place a wine and water glass at each place. Not everyone will have coffee so the coffee cups won't show up until after the meal and before the completion of the service.

This much of the table, including the candles and flowers, can be set the day before if possible.

I don't serve appetizers because of the ceremonial foods and wine served with the dinner. I usually plan to sit down at 6:30 and warn people that we will start promptly. We ask that guests arrive 30 minutes before we begin the service, which gives people a little leeway, especially when Passover falls in the middle of the week.

Brisket and Gravy (Kosher)

Over the years, I have wrestled with how much brisket I should buy per person. This cut of meat shrinks so you end up with less than you purchased. Because of this, I have finally succumbed to buying ¾-pound per person. Some years we have leftovers (which are as good, if not better, the second night) and some years not. I have found there is no way to predict how hungry your dinner guests will be, but I have always had enough.

This recipe is for 6 and can be easily tripled or even quadrupled. For our crowd of 20, I will use 16 pounds of meat. This recipe doesn't have to be an exact science. I will use three to four oven-roasting bags.

4 pounds kosher brisket (from a kosher butcher)
2 cups chopped onion (about 1 large)
3 cups chopped mushrooms, stems included
2 cups pareve vegetable broth
2 cups kosher red wine
3 tablespoons tomato paste
1 teaspoon garlic powder
1 teaspoon kosher salt (or regular if you prefer), or to taste
1 tablespoon dried thyme
2 teaspoons dried oregano
4 tablespoons potato starch (used as a thickener)
6 turns with the pepper mill, or to taste

Place all ingredients in a large roasting bag and follow directions for securing and venting the bag. Set in a large roasting pan. Turn on oven to 325 degrees and roast brisket for 3 hours. If you need to wait for guests, just turn the oven down at the 2½-hour mark to 200 degrees and let it coast. Or you can remove and let it sit in the bags for up to an hour and it will still be quite hot. For Passover, I usually make sure it comes out of the oven as we sit down to the service so I can use the oven to heat the potatoes. This recipe is great any time of year, especially on a cold winter night.

Unlike roast beef, this meat does not have to "rest" before carving. Carefully, so as not to get burned, untie the twist-tie and lift the meat to a cutting board. I find it easier to pour the gravy into a prewarmed large bowl and then fill the gravy boats from there. If you're brave and are a good shot, you can pour right into the boats. Cut the meat against the grain into thin slices. Place on large platters.

Brisket and Gravy (Nonkosher)

This recipe is great if you do not serve a kosher meal because it is so easy, makes wonderful gravy, and comes out perfect every time. If you want a lot of gravy, simply place another can of mushroom soup, dry onion mix, and wine into each of the bags.

4 pounds brisket, fat removed
1 10 3/4-ounce can golden cream of mushroom
11 ounces red wine (fill empty soup can)
1 package dry onion soup mix

Place the ingredients in a roasting bag and follow the directions for the kosher brisket noted above.

Gefilte Fish

Some families still make these fish dumplings from scratch, but I have never tried. Make sure you find out how many people will choose to have Gefilte Fish as a prelude to dinner.

1 can or jar of gefilte fish in broth (usually 6 to 8 "dumplings" per can)
1 cup water
salt, to taste
fresh ground pepper, to taste
horseradish (optional)

Pour fish into a large pan. Add about 1 cup of water, and salt and pepper. Heat slowly until hot but not boiling. Serve in a soup dish with small amount of the broth. Many people enjoy horseradish with the fish. Some families serve this dish cold.

Mashed Potatoes (Kosher)

This recipe is simple and can be prepared a day ahead of time.

1 medium-sized potato per person
1 tablespoon nondairy margarine per 4 servings
pareve creamer
salt
garlic salt
fresh ground pepper, to taste

Place potatoes in a large pan and cover with water; sprinkle with salt. Bring to a boil and cook until soft but not mushy. Drain water from potatoes and put them into a large mixing bowl. Depending on how many potatoes you used and the size of your bowl and mixer, you may need to do several batches. Add margarine and dash of garlic salt. On low speed, mix until potatoes are mashed. Begin adding about ¼ cup of the creamer and continue adding small amounts until potatoes reach the desired constancy. Add salt and pepper, to taste. Place into large casserole dishes that are ovenproof. I have several dishes that sit into a basket or holder with handles that can go right on the table. Cover with aluminum foil and refrigerate until ready to heat. About 2 hours before dinner, take the potatoes out of the refrigerator and set on the counter. One hour before dinner, place into a preheated, 350-degree oven. Bake 1 hour.

Mashed Potatoes (Nonkosher)

If not serving kosher a meal, add about 2 ounces cream cheese for each 4 potatoes. Cut into small pieces and add the cheese to the potatoes at the same time you add the butter or margarine. This is especially helpful if you are making the mashed potatoes a day ahead of time since it adds body to the potatoes when reheating them.

Steamed Broccoli

2 large head fresh broccoli
1 tablespoon butter or margarine (optional; make sure you use nondairy if cooking kosher)
juice of ½ lemon

Fresh broccoli, washed and broken into small pieces and steamed is an easy veggie to do. Of course, you can always serve frozen but I think that fresh is always the best and doesn't really take much longer to prepare.

Steam in a vegetable steamer until done to desired crispness. You can also put into a large pan with about an inch of water and cook over medium heat until done. Put in serving dish and, if desired, dab with pieces of margarine or butter and squeeze half a fresh lemon over the top. Serves 4.

Charoses

This is another dish that is required for the service. It is one of my favorite Passover treats. Plan on half an apple per person, but if you are like me and enjoy leftovers, add a few more so you'll have extra.

10 apples
1½ cups walnuts
1½ teaspoons ground ginger
1½ teaspoons cinnamon
1½ tablespoons sugar
9 tablespoons kosher red wine

Peal, core, and chop the applies into small pieces. (A food processor makes this easy.) Mix all ingredients together in a bowl, cover and refrigerate. Serves 20.

Flourless Chocolate Cake With Strawberries

Many of the recipes that I have tried for Passover are pretty boring and limited. This dessert is creamy and wonderful and easily stands alone and unadorned. (If you're a chocolate fan, this is wonderful anytime and a scoop of vanilla ice cream or a dollop of whipped cream won't hurt it! Save that treat for another day though, as it is not kosher with this meal.) Since it serves about 10 to 12, you'll need two if you are having more than 10 people. Add a few strawberries or raspberries for even more variety.

7 ounces semisweet chocolate
¾ cup pareve margarine
4 large eggs
1 1/3 cup sugar

Preheat the oven to 325 degrees. Grease and sugar an 8-inch spring form pan. Sit the pan on a large sheet of foil and form up around the outside of the pan so you can sit it in water to bake.

Melt the margarine and chocolate in a heavy medium-sized saucepan over low heat. Stir frequently and don't allow it to burn. The chocolate will melt faster if you break it into small pieces. Remove from heat. In a small bowl, whisk together the eggs and the sugar. Whisk egg mixture into the chocolate.

Pour the batter into the pan. Place the pan into a large pan (I use a roasting pan set in the oven) and add enough water to come halfway up the sides. Bake until the knife inserted into the middle comes out clean; about 75 to 90 minutes. Don't let it get overdone. It will only be about ½ to ¾ inch high. Remove from the water and let cool.

Before serving, release and remove the sides and place on a serving platter. This cake is very moist—don't even think about removing it from the bottom of the cake pan. I put a doily on the cake platter and place the cake right on top. Serve with strawberries.

Strawberries

3 pints strawberries
¼ cup Grand Marnier liqueur (or substitute 1 teaspoon sugar per pint of berries)

Timetable

The meal isn't difficult but there are a lot of preparations. While it could all be done in one day, if you were to do that, it would be very helpful to have at least one other pair of hands. Even if you do have some help, it is still much more enjoyable if you do what you can ahead of time so you aren't frazzled.

The key here is to plan your timing so as to coincide with the time you want to actually serve the meal...not with when you sit down to begin the service. In our home, the first part of the service usually lasts about 45 to 60 minutes. I plan it so the brisket comes out of the oven and the potatoes go in, just as we sit down to begin the Seder service.

1 month before Seder:
· Borrow or buy enough Haggadah and Kipat.

Weekend before:
· Shop for the nonperishable items and ingredients for Charoses.
· Plot seating assignments and make place cards.
· Find your Seder plate, Afikomen cover, and Elijah's cup.

1 day before:
· Make Charoses.
· Set table, including flowers, salt and pepper

shakers, pens, and camera.
· Make the mashed potatoes and dessert if you have time or save for tomorrow .
· Clean parsley for Seder plate and refrigerate.

Day of Seder:
· Shop for perishables early in the day.
· Make dessert.
· Make mashed potatoes, cover, and refrigerate.
· Wrap lamb shank bones and eggs separately in aluminum foil to roast in oven with meat.
· Make several cups of salt water, put in small dishes, and place on table.
· Place cushion in the leader's chair.
· Clean broccoli.
· Set serving dishes and utensils out; polish if necessary.
· Prepare gefilte fish (do not heat), cover, and refrigerate.
· Prepare strawberries and refrigerate.
· Place camera on table.
· Place pens on table, one at each end.
· Place box of matzoh at each end of table, open top.
· If necessary, run dishwasher; you'll need it to be empty.

3 hours before service begins:
· Prepare brisket and place in oven.
· Place shank bones and eggs in oven beside brisket.

- This is a good time to put your feet up for a while, rest and then prepare yourself for company.

1 hour before service:
- Remove shank bones and eggs from oven; carefully remove foil and let cool slightly.
- Prepare Seder plates; put horseradish and Charoses in separate small dishes on Seder plate along with parsley.
- Add shank bones and eggs; place Seder plates on table.
- Prepare coffeemaker but do not turn on.
- Prepare broccoli in pan and sit on top of stove (don't turn on).

30 minutes before service (guests arrive):
- Open several bottles of wine and place on table.
- Fill water glasses; put on table.
- Fill small pitcher with water (for symbolic washing of hands during service) and place with towel and bowl near to the person who will offer this to guests. Light table candles.
- Set large bowls of charoses on table.
- Fill Elijah's cup with wine and set in middle of table.
- Open sparkling cider.

Time for service to begin:
- Ask guest to find their place at table and sit down.
- Remove brisket from oven and let it set.

- Put mashed potatoes in oven at 350 degrees to warm.
- Put gefilte fish on stove, covered, and on the lowest heat possible.
- Turn on coffee pot.

Service begins:
- Light the Shabbat candles.
- Pour wine.
- Take pictures (pass camera from one end to the other).
- We have a tradition of asking our guests to sign the inside cover of the Haggadah. It's a wonderful way to remember past Seders and those who are no longer with us.
- Leader begins the service.

25 minutes into the service:
- Excuse yourself quietly and stir the gefilte fish; make sure it isn't boiling.
- Turn broccoli on at lowest heat possible.

Break for meal:
- Ask a friend or two to clear the small plates from the table. (If they are good friends, ask them to put them in the dishwasher!)
- Increase heat under broccoli if not done to your liking.
- Serve gefilte fish to those who would enjoy it. (We have a rule that newcomers have to at least try it!)
- Carefully take the brisket out of bag and slice. (My husband does this, but a guest may

wish to help here too.)

- Pour gravy into boats.
- Remove mashed potatoes from the oven and place in serving dishes
- Replenish water and wine glasses on table.
- When broccoli is ready, place into serving dishes, add butter and lemon.
- Put coffee in carafe and make second pot.
- Take all food to table.

After meal and before service resumes:

- Clear all dishes from table and put away leftovers.
- Don't be in a rush; let people sit for a while and enjoy a sip of wine.

Service resumes.

After service:

- Offer coffee.
- Serve dessert.
- Relax and enjoy! Clean up will come soon enough!

Shopping List

Check your pantry for these staples. Add those you are missing to your weekly shopping list.

____sugar

____fresh ground pepper

____ginger

____salt (kosher, if desired)

____cinnamon

____garlic salt

____garlic powder

____thyme

____oregano

____coffee

Here's what you'll need to add to your weekly shopping list:

____brisket

____lamb shank bone(s) for Seder plate

____eggs (Seder plate and dessert)

____pareve creamer (coffee, mashed potatoes)

____cream cheese (nonkosher potatoes)

____pareve margarine (broccoli, mashed potatoes, dessert)

____horseradish with beets (Seder plate, gefilte fish)

____golden cream of mushroom soup* (brisket)

____vegetable broth, pareve (brisket)

____dry, onion soup* (brisket)

____tomato paste (brisket)

____walnuts (charoses)

____semisweet chocolate (dessert)

____matzoh, kosher for Passover

____gefilte fish

____potato starch (brisket)

____potatoes (mashed potatoes)

____parsley (seder plate)

____mushrooms (brisket)

____onion (brisket)

____apples (charoses)

____strawberries (dessert)

____broccoli

____lemon (broccoli)

____oven-roasting bags (brisket)

____doily (cake plate, optional)

____flowers for the table

____candles for the table

____place cards

____sparkling cider

____kosher wine (brisket, charoses, drinking: you can use a less expensive wine for cooking)

____Grand Marnier liqueur (optional)

____film or disposable camera

*   If making the kosher brisket, obtain brisket from a kosher butcher and eliminate the mushroom and onion soups from the list.

Shopping List Amounts

The amounts on your shopping list will depend on how many you are serving for dinner. For 8 people, you'll need 2 vegetable servings of 4; for 12, you'll need 3 servings of 4; and for 16, you'll need 4 servings of 4.

To Serve:	8	12	20
brisket	6 lbs	9 lbs	16 lbs
lamb shank bone(s)	1	2 (if using 2 plates)	2 (if using 2 plates)
eggs	5	6 (for 2 plates)	6 (for 2 plates)
pareve creamer	1 1/4 cups	1 1/2 cups	2 1/2 cups
pareve margarine	3/4cup+4tablespoons	3/4cup+6tablespoons	11/2cups+11/8cups
horseradish with beets	1 bottle	1 bottle	1 bottle
golden cream of mushroom soup	2	3	5
pareve vegetable broth	4 cups	6 cups	10 cups
dry onion soup	2 packages	3 packages	5 packages
tomato paste	6 tablespoons	9 tablespoons	15 tablespoons
walnuts	1/2 cup	3/4 cup	1 1/2 cup
semisweet chocolate	7 ounces	7 ounces	14 ounces
kosher matzoh	1 box	1 box	1 box
gefilte fish	1 jar	2 jars	2 jars
potato starch	8 tablespoons	12 tablespoons	20 tablespoons
potatoes	8	12	20
parsley	1 bunch	1 bunch	1 bunch
mushrooms	6 cups	9 cups	15 cups
onion	4 cups	6 cups	10 cups
apples	4	6	10
strawberries	1 pint	2 pints	3 pints
broccoli	4	6	10
lemon	1	2	3
oven-roasting bags	2	3	4
doily	1	1	2
candles for the table place cards	8	12	20
sparkling cider	1/2 bottle per nonalcohol drinker		
kosher wine (brisket, charoses, drinking. You can use a less expensive wine for cooking.)	2 bottles for cooking plus 1/2 bottle per wine drinker	3 bottles for cooking plus 1/2 bottle per wine drinker	6 bottles for cooking plus 1/2 bottle per wine drinker
Grand Marnier	1 tablespoon	2 tablespoons	1/4 cup

DINNER FOR EIGHT: EASTER

Veggie Platter With Curry Dip
Ham With Mustard Glaze
Sweet Potatoes
Pat's Potatoes
Pear Salad
Asparagus With Shallot Sauce
Rolls
Cake With 7-Minute Frosting

Planning. The table for this traditional Easter dinner can be fun to put together. Make a centerpiece out of a large platter or basket filled with green, "Easter" grass. Fill with brightly colored eggs, chocolate bunnies, jellybeans, and other Easter goodies. Or simply use your Easter dessert cake as your centerpiece! If you have neutral or white china, use pastel tablecloth and napkins. Add pastel candles in your favorite holders and you're all set.

The meal is one you can do easily if you are pressed for tin Purchase a ham from a store such as Honey Baked Ham Company or the grocery store that is already prepared and spiral cut. To further simplify your preparations, buy fresh rolls from the bakery, as well as a cake with Easter decorations.

Tip: When preparing food for a large event, always clean as you go. Start by filling the sink with hot soapy water and wash dishes and utensils when finished with them. Not only does it keep the cleanup from being a dreaded, overwhelming process, but it keeps counters and work spaces uncluttered and clean. Remember to wash all preparation counters between foods to prevent food-borne illnesses.

Veggie Platter With Curry Dip

celery
carrots
green peppers
other favorite veggies
1½ cups sour cream (regular or lowfat)
curry powder to taste
1 tablespoon dried onion (or fresh minced)

Clean vegetables and arrange on a tray. In a small bowl, mix sour cream with 1 teaspoon curry, or to taste. Add onions, mix well, and refrigerate until serving time.

Ham With Mustard Glaze

Choose a ham based on the number of people you will be serving. Many people love to have leftovers so factor that in as well. I usually plan on 1/3 to ½ pound person. A 5- to 7-pound ham will easily feed 8 to 10 people with leftovers. It's easier to by a precooked ham because it cuts down on the baking time. Preheat oven to 350 degrees.

5 to 7 pounds precooked ham
½ cup regular mustard
½ cup packed brown sugar
½ teaspoon nutmeg
whole cloves

Mix together mustard, brown sugar, and nutmeg in a small bowl. Set glaze aside. Trim fat to no more than ¼ to ½ inch. Rinse the ham under cool water and pat dry with paper towel. Place in roasting pan and place in oven and bake allowing about 12 to 15 minutes per pound for a precooked ham. With 20 minutes left to go, remove ham from oven, pour off fat. With a knife, score the ham by cutting across the ham forming diamond shapes. This will prevent the glaze from sliding off the ham. Spoon the glaze over surface; place a whole clove in the X of each diamond. Return to oven for last 20 minutes. Remove from oven and place on serving platter.

Sweet Potatoes

Many people have their stand-by favorites for this dish. Here is the standard recipe I use for 4 to 5 people. Double the recipe if you are only serving sweet potatoes. One will be enough if you are making Pat's Potatoes.

4 medium sweet potatoes, peeled and quartered
¼ cup brown sugar, packed
¼ cup margarine
¼ cup finely chopped pecans

Place potatoes in a casserole dish, sprinkle with sugar, nuts, and "dots" of margarine. Bake in over at 350 degrees for about 45 minutes or until potatoes are soft when pierced with a fork.

Pat's Potatoes

My good friend, Pat Simmons of San Diego, shared this recipe with me. It's a great alternative if you, like me, aren't a fan of sweet potatoes.

1½ to 2 bunches sliced green onions
1 stick butter or margarine (8 tablespoons)

2 10 3/4-ounce cans cream of chicken soup
16-ounce container of sour cream (regular or
lowfat)
32 ounces shredded potatoes (frozen potatoes
are much quicker)
2 cups shredded cheddar cheese
crushed tortilla chips (or use 1 cup bread
crumbs mixed with 1 tablespoon of butter or
margarine)

Melt the butter in a Dutch oven. Add green
onions and cook until soft. Add the soup and
stir to mix. Add the sour cream; mix. Stir in the
shredded potatoes and cheddar cheese and mix
well. Put the mixture into a large casserole dish
(buttered or sprayed with vegetable spray).
Sprinkle the crushed tortilla chips on the top
and bake in a 350-degree oven for 45 minutes.

Pear Salad

(Courtesy of Kathie Davis)

This salad is so simple it's almost embarrassing.
You also have to taste it to believe that this
combination of ingredients is wonderful. The
melding of textures and flavors makes this an
easy, unusual, and delicious side dish.

Bibb lettuce, several leaves per person
½ pear, per person (2 15-ounce cans
should be plenty)
1 tablespoon mayonnaise (not
Miracle Whip), per person
1 tablespoon grated
cheddar cheese, per
person.

Wash lettuce and pat dry. On individual salad
dishes, place lettuce, topped with pear. Spoon
mayonnaise onto center of pear and top with
cheese.

Asparagus With Shallot Sauce

Small tender shoots of asparagus are at their best
in the spring so this is a perfect vegetable to serve
with Easter dinner. I plan on about 1 pound for
4 people. In the store, test one of the stalks by
snapping off an end. If it only bends and doesn't
snap off crisply, it is old. Buy green beans instead!

2 pounds asparagus
2½ cups chicken broth
½ cup white wine (optional, but add ½ cup
water if not using the wine)
2 shallots, chopped
1 tablespoon olive oil
½ cup scallions, chopped
1 tablespoon Dijon mustard
1 tablespoon lemon juice
1 teaspoon thyme or basil

Wash asparagus and remove tough end. (Simply
snap off the tough ends about 2 inches from
the bottom; if it doesn't want to break easily,
move up the spear until it snaps without effort.)
Bring broth and wine to boil in a large saucepan.
Add asparagus, cover, and simmer just until
tender and still crisp. (No longer than 3 to 4
minutes.) Remove asparagus to serving plate and
cover with foil to keep warm. Do not throw out
the broth; save 1 cup for sauce.

In a medium skillet, add oil and heat over medium flame. Add shallots and scallions and sauté until soft. Add 1 cup of the reserved broth and simmer until reduced by half. Add mustard, lemon, and thyme, and stir until smooth. Pour over asparagus.

This dish can be made a day ahead of time. Wrap asparagus in paper towels and plastic and store in refrigerator. Place sauce in a small pan and refrigerate.

Before serving, heat asparagus in microwave about 30 seconds to take off the chill and place in serving dish. Heat the sauce over a very low flame until hot. Pour over asparagus right before serving.

Rolls

Purchase rolls from the bakery or make your own. I prefer to use a box mix such as Pillsbury and like to make "horn roll" shapes. Follow directions on package. After you have kneaded the dough for the final time, roll out as directed into a circle. Cut the dough into triangular shapes, cutting from the center out. Roll each piece beginning with the wide end and roll toward the small tip. Bake according to instructions on the box. These can be made a day ahead of time but are really best if you can bake as close to dinner as possible.

For variation, our daughter Kristen sprinkles the dough with fresh chives and mozzarella cheese before rolling. You can add any herb or cheese that you wish.

Cake With 7-Minute Frosting

Make your favorite box cake in any shape you wish according to the directions. For this occasion, I prefer a yellow cake but chocolate works as well.

7-Minute Frosting
This recipe has been in the family for years and is foolproof.
1½ cups sugar
½ teaspoon cream of tarter
¼ teaspoon salt
1/3 cup water
1 tablespoon light corn syrup
2 egg whites
1 teaspoon vanilla
food coloring (optional)
shredded coconut (optional)

Add everything but the vanilla to the top of a double boiler. Place over rapidly boiling water but make sure that the top pan does not touch the boiling water. (You'll end up with an omelet.) Beat with a mixer the entire time until the frosting stands in soft peaks, usually about 7 minutes. Remove top pan from double boiler and stove. Add the vanilla and food coloring, if desired. Continue to beat until the frosting stands in stiff peaks, about 2 to 3 minutes.

Place a doily on the cake platter. If making a layer cake, place the first layer, top side down onto the platter. Frost top of cake spreading evenly. Place second layer on top but with the top side up. Frost sides first and then the top of cake with remaining frosting.

Variation: Exchange the vanilla for mint, rum, mocha, or other flavored extract.

Variation: Color the frosting green and cover the sides and top with white coconut. Decorate the top with multicolored jellybeans and yellow marshmallow chicks or bunnies. Use other Easter candies such as malt balls, shaped and colored like eggs.

Variation: I have made a sheet cake and frosted with the recipe above. Using a purchased tube of frosting (you choose the color), I outlined the shape of a bunny head and top few inches of shoulders. Outline eyes, nose, mouth, shirt, and bow tie. Use coconut, jellybeans, or other candies to decorate.

Tip: If you're like me, you have cut out numerous recipes from magazines that you have tried and want to save but don't want to copy or tape to a recipe card. Buy a large photo album that has the clear page cover that pulls back from the cardboard to allow placement of the photo. Buy some dividers and label for entrees, appetizers, desserts, salads, soups, holiday treats, and so forth. It will keep the recipes neat, tidy and handy. When you fill one book and need to start another, remove several of the categories to the new book. (For example, keep desserts and entrees in one book and appetizers, salads, and breads in the other.)

Timetable

I always like holidays that fall on a Sunday; I have Saturday to prepare. There is a great deal that can be done ahead of time for this meal preparation.

During the week before Easter:
·   If using Easter eggs for a centerpiece, purchase eggs and decoration kit.
·   Hard-boil eggs one evening, color the next, and refrigerate when dry. If you have children who are into the egg-coloring event, this can be a fun family time.

Saturday before:
·   Grocery shop early in the day.
·   Prepare veggies.
·   Make dip and refrigerate.
·   Make ham glaze and refrigerate.
·   Grate cheese for pear salad.
·   Wash lettuce leaves for pear salad and refrigerate.
·   Wash asparagus; place standing up in a container with an inch of water and refrigerate.
·   Chop shallots and scallions for asparagus.
·   If not using canned broth, make chicken broth from bouillon for asparagus and refrigerate.
·   Make cake and frost but *don't decorate;* the colors may bleed. Refrigerate. I place a few toothpicks in the cake and cover with plastic

wrap. Toothpicks will keep wrap off the frosting.
·   Set table, including salt and pepper shakers.
·   Prepare Sweet Potatoes but do not bake; cover and refrigerate.
·   Prepare Pat's Potatoes but do not bake; cover and refrigerate.
·   Determine how long the ham needs to bake and add 1 hour. (A 6-pound ham will be about 1 hour and 15 minutes.) Use this time as your benchmark for sit-down time. If dinner is at 6 o'clock, you need to begin your preparations at 3:30.

2½ hours before dinner:
·   If using Easter eggs as the centerpiece, fill large bowl with grass and add eggs and candy. Place on table.
·   If making rolls from a box mix, make dough and set aside to raise

2 hours before:
·   Preheat oven to 350 degrees
·   Shape rolls, cover with towel and let rise.
·   Depending on when guests arrive, this may be the appropriate time to bring out the veggies and dip; offer beverages.
·   Remove ham from the refrigerator, trim the fat, rinse and pat dry, place in a roasting pan.

1 hour and 45 minutes before:
·   Put ham in the oven.

1 hour before dinner:
- Assemble Pear Salad; refrigerate.
- Prepare coffeemaker but don't turn on. Grind beans for second pot.

50 minutes before:
- Put both potato dishes into oven.
- Decorate cake.
- Remove the ham from the oven, score, glaze, and insert cloves; return to oven.

45 minutes before dinner:
- Bring broth and wine to a boil and simmer asparagus for 3 to 4 minutes, until tender.
- Drain asparagus but save 1 cup of the broth.
- Place asparagus on serving platter and cover with foil.

30 minutes before dinner:
- Remove ham from oven; place on platter and cover with foil to keep warm.
- Place rolls in oven and bake until brown about 20 to 25 minutes.
- Make sauce for asparagus according to the recipe. Turn off heat and cover until serving time.

- Fill water glasses.
- If using cake as centerpiece, place on table.
- Place butter on table for rolls.

15 minutes before dinner:
- Open wine; ask someone to pour.
- Pour beverages for children or those drinking something other than wine.

5 minutes before:
- Remove potatoes from oven and place on table
- Place ham on table (Ask your guests to help.)
- Place Pear Salad at each place.
- Remove rolls from oven, put in basket, and place on table.
- Pour sauce on asparagus (warm for a minute, if necessary) and place on table.
- Light candles.
- Turn on coffee maker.
- As usual, after the meal and before serving the dessert, take a short break to clear the table, have a first cup of coffee and let the food settle.
- Enjoy!

Tip: If you wish to eat decorated Easter eggs, they shouldn't be unrefrigerated for more than 2 hours. If using them as a centerpiece, you may want to simply consider them "not for consumption."

Shopping List

Check your pantry for these staples. Add those you are missing to your weekly shopping list.

____curry powder
____mustard
____Dijon mustard
____basil
____nutmeg
____cream of tartar
____vanilla
____brown sugar
____lemon juice
____mayonnaise
____salt
____food coloring
____dried minced onions
____chicken broth
____thyme
____light corn syrup
____sugar
____coffee
____olive oil

Make sure when completing your list that you take into consideration the number of guests you are expecting and figure the amounts appropriately. Here's what you'll need to add to your weekly shopping list:

____ham
____eggs (frosting, centerpiece)
____sour cream (veggies and dip, Pat's potatoes)
____margarine (sweet potatoes, Pat's potatoes, rolls)

____cheddar cheese (pear salad and pat's potatoes); purchase already grated
____frozen shredded potatoes (Pat's potatoes)
____cake mix (dessert)
____coconut flakes (cake)
____whole cloves (ham)
____cream of chicken soup (Pat's potatoes)
____canned pears (pear salad)
____scallions (asparagus, Pat's potatoes)
____shallots (asparagus)
____Bibb lettuce (also called Boston or butterhead) (pear salad)
____asparagus
____roll mix
____tortilla chips (Pat's potatoes)
____pecans (sweet potatoes)
____sweet potatoes
____veggies (veggies and dip)
____white wine (asparagus)
____wine for drinking
____grass for table center piece
____egg decorating kit
____jellybeans (table centerpiece and cake)
____marshmallow chicks and bunnies (centerpiece, cake)
____chocolate bunnies and eggs (centerpiece)

Shopping List Amounts

If you are serving 12 guests, you'll need to double either the sweet potatoes or Pat's potatoes. You'll need another half recipe of pears and asparagus as well as 18 rolls. For 16, you'll need double recipes of pears, asparagus, and rolls, and a double recipe of either sweet potatoes or Pats potatoes.

To serve:	8	12	16
ham	5 to 7 lbs	5 to 7 lbs	6 to 8 lbs
eggs	14	14	14
sour cream	2 16-ounce packages	3 16-ounce packages	3 16-ounce packages
margarine	1 lb	2 lbs	2 lbs
cheddar cheese	2 1/2 cups	5 cups	5 1/2 cups
frozen shredded potatoes	32-ounce bag	2 32-ounce bags	2 32-ounce bags
cake mix	1 box	1 box	1 box
coconut flakes	14-ounce bag	14-ounce bag	14-ounce bag
whole cloves	small bottle or can	small bottle or can	small bottle or can
cream of chicken soup	2 cans	4 cans	4 cans
canned pears	2	3	4
scallions	3 bunches	5 bunches	5 bunches
shallots	4	6	8
Bibb lettuce	1 head	1 head	1 head
asparagus	2 lbs	3 lbs	4 lbs
roll mix	1 box	2 boxes	2 boxes
tortilla chips	small bag	small bag	small bag
pecans	1/2 cup	1/2 cup	1/2 cup
sweet potatoes	8	8	8
veggies	3 carrots, 1 pepper, 3 celery stalks, 1 jicama	add another carrot, pepper, celery stalk	add 2 more of each
white wine	1 cup	1 1/2 cups	2 cups
dinner wine	1/2 bottle per person	1/2 bottle per person	1/2 bottle per person
grass for table center piece			
egg decorating kit			
jellybeans	small bag	small bag	small bag
marshmallow chicks and bunnies			
chocolate bunnies and eggs			

DINNER PARTY FOR EIGHT

Celery With Cream Cheese and Pimientos
Shrimp With Hollandaise Sauce Over Rice
Spinach Salad
Garlic Bread
White Chocolate Angel Pie

This main dish is very rich and probably won't be enjoyed by small children as much as adults, so it's great to serve when you have a small dinner party. Because it's so rich, however, keep the appetizers light.

This recipe is easily cut in half to serve 4 or expanded to serve 12.

When setting your table, you can keep it very simple or be creative as you like. Use a tablecloth or placemats with complimentary napkins.

I always like to use candlelight and sometimes just go with simple holders and tapers and use the main dish or the breadbasket for the centerpiece. In the winter months when I don't have flowers from the garden, I often use a large clear glass bowl as the centerpiece. I put colorful rocks in the bottom, fill it three-quarters full with water and float a few candles. You can also float acorns or other nuts that are in their shells, or cranberries with the candles for a lovely fall or winter arrangement. If you choose to use a floral bouquet or arrangement, keep it low; nothing is worse than having to crane your neck over the centerpiece to see your dinner partner across the table.

Cream Cheese With Celery and Pimientos

jar of pimientos (smallest you can find)
8 ounces cream cheese, softened to room
temperature
2 tablespoons fresh chopped chives
5 stalks celery, washed and ends removed
few teaspoons milk

Blend cream cheese and chives together until smooth. Add milk, one teaspoon at a time, until the cheese is creamy. Wash celery and remove the ends, leaving the "trough" portion of the stalk. Fill with cream cheese. You can use a pastry bag with tip if you wish but it isn't necessary. Cut celery into 1-inch pieces. Top with a small piece of pimento. Place on a serving platter with a doily. Serve beside a bowl of your favorite mixed nuts. (See recipe on page 19.) Serves 8.

Shrimp With Hollandaise Sauce

The last time I made this recipe, I bought raw shrimp that were peeled and de-veined already. It cost a few dollars more a pound than the shrimp that you have to peel and clean yourself, but since there is no waste it may not be much more expensive. It sure saved time. If you decide to go this route, you only need to purchase 3 pounds of the peeled, raw shrimp. (Don't buy precooked shrimp; it will be too tough when broiled.) Warehouse stores, such as Costco and Sam's, often carry peeled raw shrimp at a very reasonable price.

4 pounds large raw shrimp or 3 pounds,
peeled and cleaned raw shrimp
2 garlic cloves, one minced and one whole
juice from a whole lemon
2 tablespoons olive oil
1 teaspoon salt
a few turns of fresh gound pepper
Hollandaise Sauce (recipe below)

Peel and de-vein shrimp. Arrange in a single layer in a dish or cookie sheet that is oven proof. Sprinkle with oil, lemon juice, salt, and pepper. Broil for about 3 to 4 minutes or just until the shrimp is pink and no longer translucent. Don't over cook or the shrimp will be tough.

Preheat oven to 400 degrees. Prepare Hollandaise sauce. (Recipe below.)

Peel the garlic cloves and cut one in half. Rub the sides and bottom of a casserole dish with the cloves. Finely chop the other clove and add to the Hollandaise sauce.

Drain the shrimp of excess oil and lemon juice and add shrimp to the casserole dish. Pour the Hollandaise sauce over them; fold gently until shrimp are covered. Put a lid or foil on the casserole and place in the oven for 10 minutes. Remove lid, turn oven to broil for about 2 minutes until top is lightly brown. Serve over rice.

This recipe can easily be adapted for 4 servings. Simply cut all ingredients in half and use only one batch of the Hollandaise sauce. The cooking instructions and baking time will remain the same.

Hollandaise Sauce

This recipe is so simple and has never failed me. I gave you the smaller proportions because I thought you would want to use this for other recipes. It is wonderful over steamed vegetables and this amount is perfect for that use. You'll need to *double this recipe* for this shrimp recipe serving eight.

3 egg yokes
2 tablespoons lemon juice
1 cup melted butter or margarine
dash of nutmeg or cayenne pepper

Separate the yokes from the egg whites. Save the whites for another use. In a blender, combine the egg yolks and lemon juice and blend until light yellow in color. Melt the butter in the microwave or on the stovetop. With the blender going, slowly add the butter in a steady stream. Add the nutmeg or cayenne pepper. I usually use margarine and it has enough salt; I never add more.

White Rice

Many people prefer fluffy rice, such as Uncle Ben's. If you are one of those, then boxed rice is probably a good way to go. Simply follow the directions on the box. Over the years, I have really come to appreciate the "sticky" rice that is preferred by the Japanese. I believe that it is more flavorful and that the texture adds another dimension to the food.

The easiest way to prepare sticky rice is to use a rice maker. There are big ones, little ones, cheap ones, and expensive ones—they all make good rice. If you have the option, the Teflon-coated pans are great because they are so much easier to clean. Follow the directions that come with the rice maker.

If you don't have a rice maker, follow the recipe below. Four cups of rice will generously feed 8 people.

4 cups white rice
4 cups cold water

A friend, who spent several years in Japan, told us that the Japanese pour the rice into the pan and put their index finger into the rice and note where it comes to on their finger. They double the height on their finger and fill the pan with water to that mark. I think it's just as easy to measure equal amounts of water and rice!

Place rice in a 4-quart pan that has a tight fitting lid. Fill pan with water to at least half full. Swirl rice and water to remove talc and pour off water. Repeat process. Some will continue to rinse until the water is clear but I get too impatient. Plus I think the talc helps to make the rice grains stick to each other. I have also heard it said that if you purchase rice without talc, you do not need to rinse at all. Add 4 cups of water, place lid on pan and bring to a boil over high heat. Reduce heat to low and simmer until almost all of the water is absorbed, about 20 minutes. Make sure lid is on tight, turn off heat and let it set for at least 15 minutes but longer is fine. Just let it set on the stove, covered, until you are ready to serve. Once the flame is turned off, *no peeking!* If you take the lid off the steam will escape and you'll have crunchy, not steamed, rice.

Spinach Salad

Dressing:
2/3 cup olive oil
¼ cup wine vinegar
2 tablespoons white wine
2 teaspoons soy sauce
1 teaspoon sugar or sugar substitute
1 teaspoon dry mustard
½ to 1 teaspoon curry
½ teaspoon garlic salt
ground black pepper, to taste

For the salad:
4 large bunches of spinach, cleaned and stems removed
10 medium mushrooms
2 hardboiled eggs, chopped
½ pound bacon fried crisp and crumbled
½ cup slivered, toasted almonds

Place eggs in cold water in a pan and place on medium heat. After the water boils, cook the eggs for 10 minutes and turn off heat. Let set for another 5 minutes and place eggs into cold water to cool. (I set the timer so I don't let them boil forever).

Mix dressing ingredients in a small bowl with a whisk or place in a bottle with a lid and shake vigorously.

Cut bacon into small pieces and fry until crisp. Drain on paper towels. Substitute the almonds for bacon if you wish, or use both. The crunch makes the salad. If using almonds, place them in a pie dish and place in a 350-degree oven for about 5 to 6 minutes or until they begin to turn brown. Mix after 3 minutes. Watch carefully; they can turn black quickly.

Spinach can be full of sand and will be very gritty if not washed thoroughly. I put the bunches in a sink full of cold water and swish. After I remove the stalk on each piece, I place the leaves in a large bowl or sieve. I then rinse out the sink thoroughly and repeat the rinsing process until there is no more sand left in the bottom of the sink. Drain well on towels. Even "prewashed" spinach that claims to be washed 3 times will still have sand and dirt on the leaves so you'll have to do it yourself at least two more times.

Peel and chop eggs. Wash and slice mushrooms. Add to bowl with spinach. Start with about ½ cup dressing (mix well before pouring on greens) and toss. Add more dressing if desired. Just before serving, garnish with bacon and/or almonds.

Garlic Bread

1½ loaves Italian bread
9 tablespoons of soft butter or margarine
6 tablespoons grated Parmesan cheese
1 whole head of garlic cloves
salt
fresh ground pepper

Preheat oven to 500 degrees.

Cut bread in half horizontally with a bread knife.

Separate the individual cloves but do not remove the "skin" from them. Heat a small skillet on medium flame and add garlic. Stir frequently for about 10 minutes until garlic begins to soften. Allow it to cool until you are able to handle the cloves; squeeze the garlic from the skins and chop into small pieces. Mix cheese, butter and garlic and mash until garlic and cheese are well distributed in the butter. Divide in thirds and spread on each half of the bread. Place on a baking sheet and into the very hot oven for about 5 minutes or until the bread is crusty on the sides and the butter is melted and starts to brown on top. Turn oven to broil and continue until top is golden brown. Remove from oven. With a bread knife, cut into pieces that are about 2 inches wide. Place a napkin in a breadbasket and top with the bread and serve.

This recipe can be easily stretched. If you have garlic bread lovers at your table, you may want to use 2 whole loaves for 8 people. Just add another 3 tablespoons of butter and 2 of Parmesan cheese and about three more cloves of garlic cloves. Follow the recipe. Remember to change the shopping list accordingly.

White Chocolate Angel Pie

This recipe is delicious and light even though it sounds rich. It's the perfect dessert to follow the rich shrimp dish and tangy salad.

Preheat oven to 275 degrees. Cut a brown paper bag or piece of parchment paper to fit a round pizza/cookie pan. Place your serving plate on bag and draw a circle with a pencil.

Meringue:
3 egg whites
¼ teaspoon cream of tartar
¾ cup sugar

Filling:
2 cups whipping cream
½ teaspoon vanilla extract
7 ounces white chocolate (preferably in block form so you can make curls for the top)
1 tablespoon cocoa for dusting top

Separate the egg whites from the yolks. Crack the egg over a separate bowl. There must not be any yolk in the whites or it will not whip correctly. By using a separate bowl, you guard against having to toss the whole thing if you have an accident with a yolk. You can use the yolks in the Hollandaise sauce or save for another recipe.

Place whites and cream of tartar in mixing bowl and beat with a mixer on high speed until very frothy. Very gradually, add the sugar in a small stream and beat until the meringue will form and hold stiff peaks.

Pour meringue onto the middle of the brown paper and with a knife or rubber spatula, shape into a resemblance of a pie pan, pushing meringue up at the edges to form sides. Leave a 1-inch border around the edge of the paper. The meringue will expand slightly and you want to ensure that it will fit on your serving plate. Bake in the middle of the oven for 1 to 1½ hours. It should be crispy and browned. Watch closely as the meringue bakes. If your oven is hotter the meringue will brown faster. Turn off the oven, open the door a notch, and let it sit in the oven for another hour. Remove from oven and let it cool completely before filling.

Place small bowl and beaters into the freezer in preparation for whipping the cream. If you are short on freezer space, about 30 minutes before whipping the cream, fill the bowl to the top with ice cubes and a little water, throw in the beaters and let sit. When ready to use, empty and dry completely with a towel to remove all of the water.

When the shell has cooled, shave about 1 ounces of white chocolate to use for curls on top of pie. I struggle with this task and have found that the easiest way for me to do this is to put the block of chocolate into the microwave for just 15 seconds to help soften it a bit and then use a potato peeler to shave off curls. Coarsely chop the remaining 6 ounces of chocolate and set aside.

In the chilled bowl, add vanilla and the whipped cream and beat until it holds firm peaks. Be careful not to over beat or you'll have butter! Gently fold in the chopped chocolate and spoon into the meringue shell. Garnish the top with the chocolate curls. Place about 1 tablespoon of cocoa in a sieve and dust the surface of the pie; you may not need the whole tablespoon. Cover with plastic wrap and refrigerate for 2 to 8 hours. Cut as you would a pie and serve with a good cup of coffee.

Tip: When beating egg whites, don't use a wood or plastic bowl. Wood can retain previous flavors and plastic contains petroleum that will prevent the whites from foaming. Make sure the bowl you use is grease free and the egg whites are free of yolk.

Timetable

The preparation time will not vary if you entertain more than 8 guests. Just allow a little more time to clean the additional shrimp and spinach and make a second dessert.

In the morning:
- Make the dessert and refrigerate.
- Boil eggs; refrigerate when cool.
- Remove cream cheese from refrigerator, cut into small pieces and place in a bowl.
- Wash celery, remove ends, and dry.
- Wash and mince chives.
- Mix cream cheese and chives; add milk as necessary.
- Stuff the celery but don't cut into pieces yet; wrap in plastic and refrigerate.
- Clean spinach, wrap in towel, and place in refrigerator.
- Pan fry garlic for bread.
- Make garlic butter.
- Peel, de-vein, and wash shrimp.
- Set the table.
- Place a napkin in the breadbasket.
- Place doily on serving platter for appetizer.

1 hour and 30 minutes before dinner:
- Make salad dressing (do not refrigerate).
- Fry bacon and drain on paper towel.
- Toast almonds.
- Place shrimp on cookie sheet and drizzle with oil, lemon, salt, and pepper.

- Wash rice, put in pan with water and cover with lid.
- Cut celery into 1-inch pieces, top with pimento and place on serving platter
- Place nuts in a bowl.
- Prepare coffee pot for first pot of coffee but don't turn on; prepare grounds for second pot and set aside.

1 hour before dinner; guests arrive:
- Serve appetizer and cocktails of choice.

30 minutes before dinner:
- Put rice on high heat and keep an eye on it so you know when it comes to a boil.
- Turn oven to broil.
- When rice has absorbed most of the water, turn off heat and let sit covered on the stove. Remember *no peeking!*
- Prepare casserole dish by rubbing sides with garlic clove.

25 minutes before dinner:
- Place shrimp under broiler for 3 to 4 minutes; don't overcook.
- When the shrimp come out of the oven, turn broiler off and turn oven to 400 degrees.
- Melt butter for Hollandaise.
- Make Hollandaise sauce

20 minutes from dinner:
- Place shrimp in casserole and fold in

Hollandaise sauce; cover with lid or foil.
· Put shrimp in oven for 10 minutes.
· Spread garlic butter on bread.
· Fill water glasses on table.

10 minutes from dinner:
· Take cover off of shrimp; turn oven to broil for 2 minutes or until top begins to brown.
· Wash and slice mushrooms.
· Open wine.

8 minutes before dinner:
· Take shrimp out of oven; turn off broiler and turn oven to 500 degrees.
· Put bread into oven and set timer for 5 minutes.
· Toss salad; start with ½ cup dressing and add more if needed. Garnish with bacon and almonds.
· Place rice in serving dish.

3 minutes before dinner:
· Check the bread; it should be hot through and the sides crusty. If not, give it another minute or two. Turn oven to broil and continue until the top of the bread is brown and bubbly
· Remove bread from oven
· Take shrimp, rice and salad to table
· Cut bread and place in serving basket; put on table.
· Turn on coffee pot.
· Pour wine.
· Call guests to the table and enjoy!

After dinner:
· Clear the dishes from the table and pour a cup of coffee. Sit for a while and enjoy your company.
· Serve the pie with a second cup of coffee and if you like, an after-dinner liqueur or port.

Shopping List

Check your pantry for these staples. Add those you are missing to your weekly shopping list.

____coffee

____cracked pepper

____white rice

____white wine

____dry mustard

____Parmesan cheese

____vanilla

____olive oil

____wine vinegar

____nutmeg

____milk

____soy sauce

____cayenne pepper

____sugar

____curry

____garlic salt

____cream of tartar

____cocoa

____salt

Here's what you'll need to buy at the store and what you'll need it for:

____uncooked shrimp with peels (shrimp with hollandaise)

____bacon (salad)

____eggs (salad, hollandaise, dessert)

____cream cheese (appetizer)

____slivered almonds (salad)

____mixed nuts (appetizer)

____whipping cream (dessert)

____small jar pimientos (celery and cream cheese)

____white chocolate in a block (dessert)

____butter (hollandaise sauce, garlic bread)

____lemons (shrimp and hollandaise sauce)

____fresh spinach (salad)

____medium mushrooms (salad)

____fresh chives (appetizer)

____celery (appetizer)

____whole heads of garlic (shrimp and bread)

____Italian bread—fresh from the bakery (garlic bread)

____wine

____soft drinks

____doily for the celery plate

Shopping List Amounts

For 4 guests, follow the shrimp recipe and use 2 pounds shrimp and 1 recipe of Hollandaise. Cut the recipes for rice, salad, and bread in half. For 12, you'll need 6 pounds of shrimp, 3 recipes of Hollandaise, and 1 1/2 recipes of rice and salad. Make 2 loaves of bread and either small servings of dessert, or make 2.

To serve:	4	8	12
uncooked shrimp with peels	2 lbs	4 lbs (3 if peeled)	6 lbs (5 if peeled)
bacon	1/2 lb	3/4 lb	1 lb
eggs*	7	11	18
cream cheese	8 ounces	8 ounces	8 ounces
slivered almonds	1/4 cup	1/2 cup	3/4 cup
mixed nuts	1 lb	1 lb	1 lb
whipping cream	2 cups	2 cups	4 cups
small jar pimientos	1	1	1
white chocolate in a block	7 ounces	7 ounces	14 ounces
butter	1 cup + 6 tablespoons	2 cups + 9 tablespoons	3 cups + 12 tablespoons
lemons	2	4	6
fresh spinach	2 bunches	4 bunches	6 bunches
mushrooms	5 medium	10 medium	15 medium
fresh chives	1 bunch	1 bunch	1 bunch
celery	5 stalks	5 stalks	5 stalks
whole heads of garlic	1 (use 1 clove for shrimp)	1 1/2 (use 1 clove for shrimp)	2 (use 1 clove for shrimp)
Italian bread—fresh from the bakery	1 loaf	2 loaves	2 loaves
wine	2 bottles +	4 bottles +	6 bottles +
soft drinks			
doily for celery plate			

*Save on eggs by using the yolks you don't use on the dessert for the Hollandaise

DINNER FOR TWELVE: SUMMER HOLIDAY BARBECUE

Shrimp Cocktail
Bleu Cheese Biscuits
Ethyl's Cream Cheese Spread
Hamburgers
Corn On the Cob
Black Bean Salad
Potato Salad
Ice Cream Pie
Iced Tea

Having friends over on a summer day can be fun and relaxing. If you are doing the whole thing yourself, it can also be a lot of work if you don't try to keep it simple. With close friends or family, don't be bashful about asking everyone to bring a dish that will help to cut down the time you spend in the kitchen.

Planning. This should be an easy event but if you want to get carried away, you can plan it around a theme of your choosing. It is a great way to celebrate a birthday and you could plan decorations accordingly and change the Ice Cream Pie to a birthday cake. Keep it simple and buy the cake at the local grocery store where they bake and decorate cakes for a very reasonable price. Use paper plates and plastic glasses and utensil for easy cleanup. I also try to keep the recipes simple to keep preparation time to a minimum. Once we sit down to eat, I like to be able to relax and enjoy the meal without having to get up and serve another course.

There are a number of options as to how you can serve this meal. Depending on the number of guests, you can either serve this buffet style or family style on a picnic table. If serving buffet style, I arrange the food on the counter in the kitchen and allow guests to take their food outdoors. That way, I don't need to be concerned about flies or other pests. If you can all gather around the picnic table, it makes conversation and second helpings much easier.

Shrimp Cocktail

It's hard to know how many shrimp to buy. A lot depends on how long between appetizers and dinner, how many shrimp lovers you have and what your budget is. I usually figure on about ¾ pound of cooked and peeled shrimp for 6 people as an appetizer.

1½ pounds cleaned and deveined shrimp

Cocktail Sauce

(See page 17 for Shrimp Cocktail and Cocktail Sauce recipes.)

Ethyl's Cream Cheese Spread

(See page 30 for recipe.)

Bleu Cheese Biscuits

(Courtesy of Kathie Davis)

2 cans ready to bake and serve biscuits (found in the dairy case at the grocery store)
½ cup (1 stick) margarine or butter
4 ounces bleu cheese
2 scallions, sliced very thin

Preheat oven to 400 degrees. Grease a 13- by 9-inch baking dish. Melt the butter in a small saucepan and then add the bleu cheese and stir until cheese is melted. Open the biscuit containers and cut each biscuit into quarters and throw into the baking dish. (Take this literally. The dough should be randomly placed in the dish.) Pour butter mixture over the dough, sprinkle with scallions. Place in oven and bake for about 20 minutes or until biscuits are baked through. Place on the table and allow guests to simply pull pieces of the bread out with their fingers. Guests rave about this dish and always want the recipe.

Hamburgers

1/3 pound ground beef, per person
cheese slices
tomatoes, sliced
onion, sliced
lettuce leaves
ketchup
mustard
mayonnaise
buns

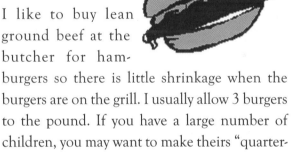

I like to buy lean ground beef at the butcher for hamburgers so there is little shrinkage when the burgers are on the grill. I usually allow 3 burgers to the pound. If you have a large number of children, you may want to make theirs "quarter-pounders." Some men will eat two, so you may want to have a few extras on hand. If you don't use them, wrap in plastic wrap and freeze for another time.

When the time comes, grill over hot coals until desired doneness, about 4 to 5 minutes a side for medium rare. This is always somewhat tricky since cooking time will vary with how hot the fire is and thick the burgers are. Add cheese for those who want cheeseburgers when burgers have about 2 minutes to go on the second side.

Serve with a tray of sliced tomatoes, lettuce, and onions. Have plenty of ketchup, mustard, and mayonnaise handy for condiments.

The rest of the dinner should be ready to go on the table when the burgers come off the grill.

Corn On the Cob

1 ear corn, per person (½ ear for small children)
butter or margarine
salt
fresh ground pepper

I prefer white corn rather than yellow but it truly is a matter of personal choice and what's available in your area. I try to always buy the corn on the day of the event so it is as fresh as possible. If you're in an area where corn is grown, you may have the luxury of going to roadside stands where you can be assured it has

been recently picked—sometimes just hours before.

There are probably as many ways to cook corn on the cob as there are recipes for turkey dressing. I use the following method because it's very easy and is a no-brainer with respect to the rest of the preparations.

Keep corn in the refrigerator wrapped in a wet towel. Shuck immediately before cooking. I often have guests do this for me while I'm putting the last-minute touches on the meal. Clean all silk from the ears and cut off any stalk. Bring a large pot of water to a boil. Add corn, cover with lid, and as soon as it comes to a boil again, turn off heat and let it remain covered until ready to serve. You don't need to worry about overcooking with this method and it always comes out tender.

Serve hot with butter, salt, and pepper. If you happen to have any leftovers, cut it from the cob, place in a freezer bag, and freeze to use in soups or in the Black Bean Salad that follows.

Tip: Don't shuck corn on the cob until right before cooking time. It's best not to even peek in the top when purchasing as the corn begins to toughen when the kernals hit the air.

Black Bean Salad

(Courtesy of Connie Krall)

1 15-ounce can black beans, rinsed
1 15-ounce can corn
½ green bell pepper, cut into small pieces
½ sweet red pepper, cut into small pieces.
¼ cup minced onion, cut very small)
½-cup flavored vinegar (You can use any vinegar and oil salad dressing. I prefer Consorzio Mango Fat Free Dressing and Marinade that I find at stores such as Williams-Sonoma or specialty wine and cheese stores.)

Mix together, preferably a day ahead so the flavors have a chance to meld. Cover and refrigerate. Serves 6 to 8.

Potato Salad

Here's another dish that has hundreds of variations. This is my mother's recipe and I like it best.
5 medium russet potatoes
2 eggs
¾ cup diced celery
½ cup minced onions
½ teaspoon celery seed
1 cup mayonnaise or salad dressing (such as Miracle Whip)
1 tablespoon mustard
½ teaspoon sugar

Place the eggs in a small pan and cover with water. Bring to a boil and cook for about 8 minutes. Turn off the heat and allow to sit for about 10 minutes. Pour off water and cover with cold water to cool.

Place potatoes in a pan, cover with water, and bring to a boil until they are cooked through but not real soft. (If you overcook, they will become mushy and you'll end up with a dish that is more like flavored mashed potatoes.) Remove from water and allow to cool. (This can be done the day before you assemble the salad.) Peel potatoes and cut into small pieces.

In a small bowl, mix together the mayonnaise, mustard, sugar, and celery seed. (If using regular mayonnaise instead of Miracle Whip, add a tablespoon of vinegar.)

Place the rest of the ingredients in a large bowl and mix in the dressing. Cover and refrigerate. Serves 6 to 8.

When ready to serve, garnish dish with parsley, black olive, tomatoes, or other herbs, if desired.

Tip: Watch for ground beef specials at the grocery store. You can buy the meat, make into patties, and freeze for use at a later time. It's not only economical, but it will save you the time of making the patties on the day of the barbecue.

Ice Cream Pie

This recipe is simple and allows for a great deal of variation. My favorite is Oreo cookies with mint chip ice cream and chocolate syrup. You are only limited by your imagination. For variety, you can use vanilla wafers and different flavors of ice cream and syrups. You could even add some surprises between the layers such as candy pieces, chocolate chips, or nuts.

One 10-inch pie can serve as many as 10 to 12, but you may need 2 if you have all adults with big appetites.

½ package Oreo cookies
½ gallon ice cream
chocolate syrup

Allow ice cream to sit at room temperature for about 15 minutes before you assemble the pie.

Line a pie pan with whole cookies including the sides to form a pie "shell." Spoon about half of the ice cream into the shell and drizzle syrup over the surface. Add remaining ice cream. Cover with plastic wrap and place in the freezer until ready to serve. It is best to make this dessert at least 8 hours before serving so the ice cream gets hard again. Right before serving, drizzle the top with more syrup. Serve with coffee.

Iced Tea

1 gallon water
3 tea bags

Put water in a large pan and place on stove to heat. As soon as steam starts to rise, turn off the heat and put in 3 of your favorite tea bags. Let steep for about 45 minutes to 1 hour. Remove bags and place in container or pitcher in the refrigerator to cool.

Tip: If you are a garage sale junkie, watch for candlestick holders that are missing their partner. Loners can be mixed with different length tapers to make very unusual centerpieces. Wrap wide ribbon around and through the candlesticks or use greens or flowers at the base to close the gaps between the holders.

Timetable

A week to several days before the barbecue:

- You can do your grocery shopping for everything except the ears of corn, ground beef, shrimp (unless you plan to buy frozen shrimp), produce, and buns.
- Make the ice cream pie and freeze.

1 day before:

- Make the Cocktail Sauce and refrigerate.
- Make Ethyl's Cream Cheese Spread; refrigerate.
- Chop onion and celery for Potato Salad at the same time you are chopping the onions and peppers for bean salad and refrigerate; if you have time, make Potato Salad and refrigerate.
- Make the Black Bean Salad and put in serving dish; refrigerate.
- Boil the potatoes and refrigerate when cool.
- Chop 2 scallions for Bleu Cheese Biscuits; refrigerate.
- Make iced tea; refrigerate.

Early in the day of the barbecue:

- Peel potatoes and finish making the salad, place in its serving dish, and refrigerate.
- Finish grocery shopping.
- Make hamburger patties and refrigerate.
- Clean up your outside area, make sure tables and chairs are cleaned off.
- Prepare plates, napkins, utensils, and cups.
- Select platters and serving utensils for the corn and hamburgers, basket for the

crackers, dish for the shrimp.
- Slice onions and clean lettuce for hamburgers and store separately in plastic bags in refrigerator.
- Defrost shrimp and refrigerate.

3 hours before guests begin to arrive:

- Place soft drinks, beer, and wine in cooler with ice.
- Take time for yourself to relax, then dress for the occasion.

45 minutes before guests arrive:

- Melt butter and bleu cheese for Bleu Cheese Biscuits in a small pan and take off stove.
- Use the foil wrapper from the butter to grease the baking dish. Take biscuits out of container and cut each into quarters, placing in the dish.
- Add bleu cheese to butter and stir until it melts.
- Prepare the bar. Put ice in bucket and cut a few lemon or lime slices, if desired.
- Place crackers in a basket.
- Preheat oven for biscuits.
- Prepare coffeemaker but don't start.

15 minutes before guests:

- Reheat the butter and cheese mixture and complete biscuit recipe, placing the biscuits in oven to bake.
- Crush ice to put in bottom of shrimp dish.
- Remove Cream Cheese Spread and Cocktail Sauce from refrigerator.

When guests arrive:

· Place the shrimp over the ice and serve along with the Cream Cheese Spread and crackers.

· Offer drinks to guests. About the time you've finished serving the first round of beverages, the biscuits should be coming out of the oven. Serve the biscuits, then relax.

About 60 minutes before dinner:

· If using a charcoal grill, light the coals and allow them to progress to gray, glowing coals.

About 45 minutes before:

· Have friends shuck corn.

· Place a large pot of water on stove and bring to a boil.

· Wash corn and remove any silk; add to water, as soon as it comes to a boil and cover with lid. When it comes to a boil again, turn off heat, and let it sit until ready to serve.

30 minutes before:

· If using a gas grill, turn in on now.

20 minutes before:

· Assemble the utensils, paper plates, napkins, salt and pepper, and condiments for hamburgers (ketchup, mustard, and mayonnaise) and place on table.

· Slice tomatoes and place with sliced onions and lettuce on a tray and place on table.

· Turn on coffeemaker.

15 minutes before:

· Place burgers on the grill and cook until desired doneness, about 4 to 5 minutes per side for medium-rare. Add cheese slices for the last 2 minutes. If guests prefer toasted buns, place on grill at the same time you add the cheese.

· Place coffee in a thermos and prepare a second pot but don't turn on.

5 minutes before:

· Place salads and corn butter on the table.

· Remove corn from water and put on a large patter; place on table.

· Suggest that guests refresh their beverages before dinner.

Dinner time:

· Place all food on table.

· Call guests to go through the line.

· Turn on the second pot of coffee and enjoy!

Dessert time:

· Clear the table and put leftovers away.

· Don't rush toward dessert. Allow everyone to sit, relax, and let dinner settle before offering the next course. Guests may even like to have a cup of coffee before finishing off the meal with something sweet.

· Remove ice cream pies from the freezer and allow to sit for a few minutes to make serving easier.

· Place sugar and cream or milk for coffee on table. Allow guests to serve themselves.

· Refresh the coffee as needed.

Shopping List

Check your pantry for these staples. Add those you are missing to your weekly shopping list.

____ketchup

____mustard

____mayonnaise

____Worcestershire sauce

____poppy seeds

____celery seed

____salt

____pepper

____sugar

____tea

____coffee

Here's what you'll need to add to your weekly shopping list:

____cleaned and deveined shrimp (appetizer)

____ground beef (hamburgers)

____margarine or butter (corn and bleu cheese biscuits)

____bleu cheese (bleu cheese biscuits)

____cream cheese (cheese spread)

____American or other cheese (hamburgers)

____eggs (potato salad)

____chocolate syrup (ice cream pie)

____Oreo cookies (ice cream pie)

____crackers (cheese spread)

____buns (hamburgers)

____horseradish (cocktail sauce)

____large green olives with pimientos (cheese spread)

____black beans (bean salad)

____corn (bean salad)

____Consorzio Mango Fat Free Dressing and Marinade (bean salad)

____biscuits (bleu cheese biscuits)

____ice cream (dessert)

____celery (potato salad)

____large red onion (hamburgers)

____tomatoes (hamburgers)

____lettuce (hamburgers)

____large onion (potato salad, bean salad)

____red pepper (bean salad)

____green pepper (bean salad)

____corn on the cob

____scallions (bleu cheese biscuits)

____lemon (shrimp cocktail sauce)

____potatoes (potato salad)

____beverages (soft drinks, beer, wine, iced tea, milk)

____paper plates, napkins, utensils and glasses/cups

____bags of ice, if needed

Shopping List Amounts

The recipes in this section serve 6, so double the recipes for the bean salad, potato salad, and dessert for both 12 and 16 guests.

To serve:	8	12	16
shrimp	1 lb	1 1/2 lbs	2 lbs
ground beef	3 lbs	4 1/2 lbs	6 lbs
margarine or butter	1/2 lb	3/4 lb	3/4 lb
bleu cheese	4 ounces	4 ounces	4 ounces
cream cheese	8 ounces	8 ounces	8 ounces
American or other cheese	8 slices	12 slices	16 slices
eggs	2	4	4
chocolate syrup	1 bottle	1 bottle	1 bottle
Oreo cookies	1 bag	2 bags	2 bags
crackers	1 box	1 box	1 box
buns	8	12	16
horseradish	small bottle	small bottle	small bottle
large green olives with pimentos	¾ cups, sliced	¾ cups, sliced	¾ cups, sliced
black beans	1 15-ounce can	2 15-ounce can	2 15-ounce can
corn	1 15-ounce can	2 15-ounce can	2 15-ounce can
Consorzio mango dressing	1 bottle	1 bottle	1 bottle
biscuits	2 cans	2 cans	2 cans
ice cream	1/2 gallon	1 gallon	1 gallon
celery	3/4 cup, diced	1 1/2 cup, diced	1 1/2 cup, diced
red onion	1 large	2 large	2 large
onion	1 large	2 large	2 large
tomatoes	2	2	3
lettuce	1 head	1 head	1 head
red pepper	1	1	1
green pepper	1	1	1
corn on the cob	8 ears	12 ears	16 ears
scallions	1 bunch	1 bunch	1 bunch
lemon	1 plus garnish	1 plus garnish	1 plus garnish
potatoes	5	10	10
soft drinks	at least 1 per person but more for nonalcohol drinkers		
beer	2 beers per beer-drinking person		
wine	1/2 bottle per wine-drinking person		
paper plates			
napkins			
utensils			
glasses/cups			
ice, if needed			

DINNER FOR SIX: SUMMER DINNER PARTY

Veggies and Dip
Assorted Cheeses, Crackers, and White Grapes
Grilled Leg of Lamb
Grilled Vegetables
Corn On the Cob
Onion Bread
Homemade Ice Cream With Fresh Berries
Iced Tea

There isn't much I enjoy more than having a few friends over for a summer barbecue. What better way to spend a warm summer evening than to be outside listening to summer sounds and smell great food cooking on the grill! It's especially fun when you keep the menu simple and chose things that keep you out of the kitchen when it's hot.

Planning. Most of the cooking is done after your guests have arrived. It also allows a great deal of flexibility since most of the main meal is cooked at the same time on the grill and everything else can be prepared ahead of time. If you have a picnic or other table outside, plan to spend the entire evening outdoors.

You can use your everyday dishes and tablecloth or place mats. If you wish, can use paper plates but get the plastic ones that won't get soggy or cause problem when cutting the meat.

I like a lot of candlelight, but you'll probably need kerosene-type lanterns, small votive candles, or hurricane lamps that go over your regular candlestick holders. Otherwise, the wind will blow out the flames or cause the wax to spray over the holders and table setting. Also, if bugs are a problem in you areas, you may want to strategically place citronella candles around the area keep them at bay.

I try to keep the appetizer portions small so guests aren't full before we sit down to dinner. Serve with your favorite cocktail, wine, or freshly brewed sun tea.

Veggies and Dip

celery
carrots
green peppers
1 cup sour cream
soy sauce, to taste

Because you're going to have a lot of vegetables with the meal, wash and cut into dipping size just a few and refrigerate until serving time. Make it really simple by purchasing veggies already cleaned and cut. Of course, you can use your favorite dip or even just put out a bowl of you favorite ranch-style salad dressing. One of our favorites is easy and always gets rave reviews. Add soy sauce to the sour cream, starting with about 1 tablespoon of soy sauce. Add small amounts until the sour cream is a light brown color and has a rich taste. Refrigerate until serving time.

Assorted Cheeses, Crackers, and White Grapes

8 to10 ounces Brie or Camembert cheese
several bunches of seedless white grapes (red can be used, also)
crackers

Select a small wedge of cheese such as Brie or Camembert and serve with your favorite crackers and a few bunches of firm white grapes. Let the cheese sit out for about an hour before serving so it softens and is easy to spread. Put all on a large platter and allow guests to serve themselves.

Grilled Leg of Lamb

3- to 4-pound leg of lamb (off the bone), butterflied
1 cup red wine
1 cup lemon juice (bottled or fresh)
1 cup soy sauce
6 garlic cloves, minced
1 tablespoon dried basil
1 tablespoon dried oregano
1 tablespoon dried rosemary (crush with your fingers as you add to the marinade)
3 to 4 good turns of the pepper mill

Buy a leg of lamb from the butcher and ask them to de-bone and "butterfly" it so it will lie flat on the grill. Sometimes, you can find a prepackaged one at warehouse grocery stores, where the prices are very reasonable.

The lamb should marinade overnight in the refrigerator, but if you run out of time, let it marinade for at least for 8 hours the day of your dinner. Rinse the meat under cool water, pat dry, cut off the excess fat, and place in a large plastic bag (such as a small trash bag) along with the other ingredients.

Mix well and tie the end in a knot close to the meat. Place the bag in a bowl in the refrigerator. Turn occasionally.

About 30 minutes before grilling time, light the barbecue. Remove the meat from the bag and discard the marinade. If you are using charcoal, start the fire 60 minutes earlier so the coals are hot with a gray ash and not flaming. Place the meat on the grill and close the lid. Check frequently so it doesn't flame up. Grill for about 15 minutes on one side and turn. After another 15 minutes, turn again. Because this is a thick cut of meat, it may take about 40 to 45 minutes on the grill for medium-rare. Check frequently so you don't overcook. Keep the flames low and savor the lovely aroma while you're waiting!

Just as with beef, lamb needs to "rest" for about 10 to 15 minutes when it comes off the grill and will continue to cook while it sits. For medium rare, take it off the grill when the internal temperature is about 150 degrees.

Variation: This marinade can also be used with beef to make a great Carne Asada. Simply omit the rosemary and add an additional tablespoon of oregano. You can use London broil, flank steak, chuck, or sirloin. Grill to desired doneness and let rest for 10 minutes before carving into very thin slices on the diagonal.

Grilled Vegetables

½ artichoke, per person
½ potato, per person
1 large eggplant
4 mushrooms, per person
zucchini (optional)
tomatoes (optional)
green beans (optional)

Marinade

1/3 cup balsamic vinegar
1 cup olive oil
2 cloves garlic, minced
1 tablespoon dried basil
1 to 2 good turns of the pepper mill
butter or mayonnaise (optional)
sour cream (optional)

You can grill just about any vegetable you like, but our favorites are artichokes, potatoes, mushrooms, and eggplant. If you do zucchini, green beans, and tomatoes, I suggest you tie about 4 beans together in a bunch and put cherry tomatoes and mushrooms on skewers. The marinade can be made up to 3 days ahead and stored in the refrigerator. You'll need to bring it to room temperature before adding the vegetables. You can marinate the veggies anywhere from 2 to 8 hours.

To prepare the artichokes: Cut off stem and remove small tough row of leaves around the bottom of the choke. Use scissors and cut off the prickly points of the leaves.Rinse under water, then cut in half lengthwise. Place about 1½ inches of water in the bottom of a double boiler and set the artichokes in the top of the boiler, bottom side down. Cover with lid and steam until chokes are tender but not mushy, about 45 minutes. (If they are overdone they will come apart on the grill.) I like to eat the artichokes as they are right off the grill but some guests may like to have a little butter or mayonnaise on the side for dipping.

To prepare the potatoes: While the chokes are steaming, wash about 4 medium potatoes, place in a pan, cover with water, and bring to a boil. Cook until they are just tender when pierced with a fork, about 20 minutes. Again, if they are overcooked, they will be mushy and fall through the grill. Remove from the heat, pour off hot water, and cover with cold water until they can be handled. Remove skin and slice lengthwise and about ½ inch wide. Some people may enjoy a little sour cream on the side; you can add some fresh chopped dill or thyme for variation.

To prepare the mushrooms: Wash and cut off bottom of stem.

To prepare the marinade: You'll need to make two separate batches, one for the artichokes and one for the other veggies.

In a large Ziploc bag, prepare the marinade and add the artichokes. Seal the bag and turn to coat all sides of chokes. Lay flat in the refrigerator and turn over from time to time.

In another Ziploc bag, make another batch of the marinade; add the potatoes, zucchini, beans, tomatoes, and mushrooms. Seal the bag and turn to coat the vegetables. Lay flat in the refrigerator and turn occasionally. Place about 4 mushrooms on each skewer so the mushroom caps will lie flat on the grill right before grilling. (Soak the wood skewers in water for about 30 minutes before use.)

To prepare the eggplant: Do not marinate with the rest of the veggies, as it will get soggy. About 1 hour before grill time, wash the eggplant and cut into slices that are about ½-inch thick. Place on a paper towel and salt lightly. Turn over and salt the other side as well. Just let them set. When you remove the other veggies from the bags, save the marinade in a dish. You will use this to baste the eggplant and other veggies on the grill. Prior to grilling, cut pieces in half. Pat dry with a paper towel. Place all vegetables on the grill; turn when grill marks appear on a side and remove when heated through.

Corn On the Cob

See recipe on page 92.

Tip: Watch for meat sales at the grocery store. Meat will freeze well for up to two months, so don't buy more than you can use in that time period. When hamburger is on sale—especially during the summer—buy several pounds and make into hamburger patties. Freeze in individual or small packages that can be pulled out for an impromptu BBQ.

Have more than you can use by Labor Day? Thaw and make a pot of chili for the coming fall months.

Onion Bread

1 loaf French bread
1/8 cup minced onion
½ cup soft butter or margarine

This meal provides such wonderful juices that it seems a shame not to have bread for sopping up. However, you will certainly have enough food without it so it is truly optional. This is a great change from the traditional garlic bread.

Mix 1/8 cup minced onion with ½ cup of soft butter or margarine. Slice a large loaf of French or sourdough bread, about ¾ inches thick slices but don't cut through to the bottom. Spread the butter on one side of each slice of bread and wrap tightly in aluminum foil. Heat oven to 350 degrees and bake bread for about 15 to 20 minutes or until heated through and butter is melted. Of course, you can always buy a loaf of prepared garlic bread at the store and just follow the directions on the bag. If your have a large grill, you can place the bread on the grill to heat; turn frequently.

If you like your bread a little more toasted, you can slice the bread into pieces, butter with the mixture and place on a cookie sheet and broil in the oven for about 5 minutes or until browned. To add even more variety for another time, sprinkle with a little Parmesan cheese before putting it under the broiler.

Variation: Substitute minced garlic for the onion for garlic bread.

Homemade Ice Cream With Fresh Berries

4 egg yokes
1 cup sugar
4 cups whipping cream
1 vanilla bean or 2 teaspoons vanilla extract

In a saucepan, beat egg yolks well and mix in sugar and 3 cups of whipping cream. Cut the vanilla bean open and scrape out the seed and put them, along with the bean, into the egg and cream mixture. Cook over low heat until mixture begins to thicken and coats a metal spoon. Remove the vanilla bean. Cool to room temperature. Add one more cup of cream. Freeze according to the directions on the ice cream maker. Ice cream should be made at least 4 hours ahead of time so it can harden in the freezer.

If you don't want to mess with the vanilla bean, use vanilla extract but add it when you add the last cup of cream. If you do otherwise, your ice cream may be bitter tasting.

I love homemade ice cream and with today's electric ice cream makers, it's very easy. However, if you're not up to the fuss, buy your favorite brand.

Variation: For chocolate (or mint), melt 1 cup of chocolate chips (or mint chips) and add to the custard with the last cup of whipping cream. Continue with basic recipe.

Variation: For strawberry or peach, cut 2 cups fresh fruit into small pieces and sprinkle with 2 tablespoons sugar. Lightly mash with a fork to release the flavor and juices and let stand for about 30 minutes. Add to custard when adding the last cup of cream. Continue with basic recipe.

Variation: Toast pecan pieces in a little butter, salt lightly, and add to chocolate ice cream. When the ice cream is almost done, add nuts slowly through the hole in the top of the ice cream maker.

Variation: For chocolate chip ice cream, melt chocolate chips in the microwave until very hot and smooth. When vanilla ice cream is almost done, pour chocolate slowly through the top of the maker. It will quickly harden and become dispersed throughout the cream.

Variation: Add any other kind of goodies such as peanuts, M&M's, broken bits of Heath Bar, smashed peppermint candies, and so forth, to any flavor at the end stage. Be creative!

Fresh Berries

3 cups fresh sliced strawberries or other berries (1 pound whole berries, cleaned and sliced, is approximately 2 cups)
4 tablespoons Grand Marnier liqueur (optional)

Wash and pick over berries. If using strawberries, slice into small pieces. I like to pour about 4 tablespoon of Grand Marnier or other orange-flavored liqueur over the berries and let sit for a few hours; mix occasionally. If you'd rather not use the liqueur, add ¼ cup orange juice and sprinkle with 2 tablespoons of sugar; let sit as above.

At serving time, place a generous scoop of ice cream into each dish and top with ½ cup berries.

Iced Tea

1 gallon water
3 tea bags
sugar (optional)
lemon (optional)

Put water in a large pan and place on stove to heat. As soon as steam starts to rise, turn off the heat and put in 3 of your favorite tea bags. Let steep for about 45 minutes to 1 hour. Remove bags and place in container or pitcher in the refrigerator to cool.

Serve with sugar and/or lemon, if desired.

Tip: If you are making a salad for a large number of people and don't have a bowl that's large enough to toss the ingredients without getting lettuce all over the place, use a trash liner! The salad with dressing always becomes a little more compact and will look nice and tidy once it is put in a bowl.

Timetable

Although the majority of this meal will be prepared on the day of dinner, I like to try and do even little things through the week that will help to give some relief on the day of the party.

1 week before dinner:
- Purchase leg of lamb (check date and freeze, if necessary)
- Shop for the nonperishables
- You can make the ice cream ahead of time and keep in the freezer, or wait until party day.

2 days before:
- Make 2 batches of the veggie marinade and refrigerate

1 day before:
- Make sour cream dip for veggies and refrigerate
- Prepare lamb, place in marinade and refrigerate (remember to turn occasionally)
- Make iced tea

The morning of the dinner:
- Shop for fruits and vegetables
- Prepare artichokes, potatoes, and mushrooms, and put in marinade (refrigerate and turn occasionally)
- Make ice cream and place in the freezer
- Clean veggies for appetizer and place in baggies in the refrigerator
- Wash grapes.

- Clean berries, add Grand Marnier or orange juice and sugar; refrigerate.
- Make onion butter, prepare bread, wrap in aluminum foil; refrigerate.

3 hours before:
- Put your feet up or take a relaxing bath and get ready to entertain.

2 hours before:
- Set the table, including candles and lighting.
- Prepare bar, cocktail napkins, and so forth.
- Put crackers in basket.
- Place cheeses and grapes on serving tray.
- Place veggies and dip on serving tray.
- Prepare coffeemaker but don't turn on.
- Wash and slice eggplant, pat dry, and salt.

1 hour and 45 minutes before:
- If using charcoal grill, light fire.

1½ hours before (guests begin to arrive):
- Serve cocktails and appetizers.

1 hour and 20 minutes before:
- If using gas grill, preheat.
- Remove meat from marinade; discard the liquid.
- Put wood skewers in water to soak.

1 hour before:
- Put meat on grill, cover with lid. Watch carefully so it doesn't flare up.

45 minutes before:
· Fill large pot with water for corn, cover with lid, and bring to boil.
· Put bread in oven at 350 degrees or place on side of grill to warm.
· Turn meat as needed.
· Shuck corn.
· Remove veggies from marinade and reserve liquid.
· Place mushrooms on skewers.

30 minutes before:
· Turn meat (and bread, if on grill).
· Put veggies on grill.

20 minutes before:
· Check meat. At this point you really have to adjust you plan based on whether the meat has reached the appropriate level of doneness for your liking. Remember you should let it "rest" for about 10 minutes before carving, and it will continue to cook a little while it sits so it should come off the grill when it is a little more rare. If it's already where you want it to be, remove from grill and carve immediately; cover with foil until the rest of the meal is ready.
· Place corn in water, cover, and let it come to a boil again. Immediately turn off and let it sit.
· Turn veggies...watch them closely so they don't burn. Baste with reserved marinade.

· Check bread.
· Melt about ½ cup butter to serve with artichokes, if desired.

10 minutes before:
· Turn and baste veggies.
· Ask one of your guests to thinly slice the meat.
· Light candles on table.
· Remove appetizer dishes.
· Pour water and beverages.
· Place butter for corn on table.

5 minutes before:
· Take veggies off grill; put onto serving platter.
· Remove corn from water.
· Place bread in basket.

Dinner time:
· Ask guests to be seated.
· Put all dishes on the table, including hot butter for artichokes.
· Turn on the coffeemaker.

Dessert time:
· Relax. After everyone is finished with the main meal, pour another glass of wine or ice tea, offer a cup of coffee and clear the table. Then just rest for a while and let things settle.
· When people feel like they are ready for a little something sweet, serve dessert, and another cup of coffee. Enjoy the summer night!

Shopping List

Check your pantry for these staples. Add those you are missing to your weekly shopping list.

_____ soy sauce

_____ garlic cloves

_____ dried basil

_____ dried rosemary

_____ dried oregano

_____ fresh ground pepper

_____ salt

_____ sugar

_____ balsamic vinegar

_____ olive oil

_____ vanilla

_____ coffee

_____ tea

Here's what you'll need to add to your weekly shopping list:

_____ leg of lamb

_____ sour cream (dip and potatoes)

_____ eggs (ice cream)

_____ whipping cream

_____ margarine (artichoke dip, onion bread, corn)

_____ cheese, such as Camembert, Brie, or Swiss

_____ crackers (cheese and crackers)

_____ vanilla bean (ice cream)

_____ French or sourdough bread

_____ lemon juice (marinade)

_____ carrots (veggies and dip)

_____ celery (veggies and dip)

_____ green or red pepper (veggies and dip)

_____ artichokes (grilled veggies)

_____ mushrooms (grilled veggies)

_____ russet potatoes (grilled veggies)

_____ eggplant

_____ corn on the cob

_____ small white onion (onion bread)

_____ other veggies for grilling, if desired

_____ white grapes (cheese and crackers)

_____ strawberries, blueberries, or raspberries (ice cream)

_____ orange juice (fruit for ice cream, optional)

_____ red wine (marinade)

_____ wine, soft drinks (beverage)

_____ wooden skewers (mushrooms)

_____ Grand Marnier liqueur

Shopping List Amounts

You'll need to double all the recipes for 12 guests with the exception of the cheese.
Three wedges should be plenty.

To serve:	6	12
leg of lamb	1 3- to 4-lb leg	2 3- to 4-lb leg
sour cream	2 cups	4 cups
eggs	4	8
whipping cream	4 cups	8 cups
margarine	2 cups	4 cups
cheese (Camembert, Brie, Swiss)	2 wedges	3 wedges
crackers	1 box	1 box
vanilla bean	1 bean	2 beans
French or sourdough bread	1 loaf	2 loaves
lemon juice	1 cup	2 cups
carrots	2	4
celery	2 stalks	4 stalks
green or red peppers	1	2
artichokes	3	6
mushrooms	24 large	48 large
russet potatoes	4 medium	8 medium
eggplant	1 large	2 large
corn on the cob	6 ears	12 ears
white onion	1/8 cup	1/4 cup
other veggies	if desired for grilling	if desired for grilling
white grapes	1 bunch	2 bunches
strawberries, blueberries, or raspberries	1 1/2 lbs	3 lbs
orange juice	1/4 cup	1/2 cup
red wine	1 cup	2 cups
wine	1/2 bottle per wine drinker	
wooden skewers	1 package	1 package

DINNER FOR SIXTEEN: BRUNCH

Breakfast Strata
Fruit Salad
Mixed Green Salad With Cucumber and Dill Dressing
Rolls
Chocolate Cake and Ice Cream
Iced Tea With Mint Sprigs

Whether you are celebrating a bridal or baby shower, graduation, baptism or brit, a simple meal that can be prepared in advance allows you to attend a ceremony and get the meal on the table with minimal attention. You can then join your guests and enjoy the rest of the day. This simple menu can be made easier if you buy some prepared foods.

Planning. Depending on how many people attend your celebration, you can serve a sit-down brunch or buffet table. Think about a garden party if the weather is warm and predictable—but have a backup plan if summer showers move in. You can always rent tables and chairs to use inside or out. Linens as well as china and glasses are also available and the expense is sometimes well worth it...especially considering that you won't have to do dishes or laundry!

Your decorations will also be determined by the season and the event. Freshly cut flowers can be simple, pretty, and inexpensive centerpieces. You can leave as is or use small plastic "props" such as baby bottles and rattles for a baby shower, brit, or baptism. Add a bride and groom or wedding bells for a bridal shower. If it's an event where gifts are expected, leave the center of the table bare and allow a few of the smaller gifts to be the centerpiece. Or use your decorated cake with some cut flowers tucked around the base of the cake.

If you are serving a large number of guests and wish to use "paper" plates, make sure they are plastic or the sturdy sort of paper that can withstand liquid. I prefer linen tablecloths rather than paper even if using paper plates and plastic utensils. They add a touch of stability and won't fly around outside or dissolve when wet.

If serving buffet style, place plates, napkins, and utensils first, followed by the main dish, salads, and rolls. I always place the beverages at the end of the line and make sure there is space for the guest to set their plate while fixing their beverage.

If you choose buffet style, it is helpful to have trays the guest can sit on their lap to accommodate a plate and glass. Serve foods that are easy to cut and handle. (Have you ever tried to cut roast beef while balancing a plate on your knees?) Throw a blanket or two under a tree and let the kids sit on the ground.

You can choose to make and do everything "from scratch," or you can purchase fruit salad that is already prepared, greens for the salad that are ready to rinse and serve, fresh rolls, and a decorated cake from the bakery. Purchase orange juice that comes in a bottle and simply pour into pitchers ahead of time. You could even substitute purchased quiche Lorraine for the Strata, ready to heat and serve, from your favorite deli or grocery.

Our experience is that people aren't in the mood for big appetizers before brunch, but especially if I'm serving mimosa or champagne, I like to at least put out a bowl of mixed nuts. Place orange juice in pitchers the day before so it is cold. Allow guests to help themselves to iced tea, champagne, and orange juice while the Strata is baking and you complete the rest of the preparations.

Tip: Looking for an unusual wedding or bridal shower gift? Fill a basket with cooking staples—dried herbs and spices, olive oil, flavored vinegars, rock salt, whole pepper corns, mustards, whole vanilla beans, cocoa, food coloring, Worcestershire sauce, nutmeg seeds and grater, fresh garlic rope (they keep for months), and so forth.

Another good gift idea is to copy several of your favorite recipes onto cards and purchase all of the necessary nonperishable ingredients included in the recipes. Place in a basket with place mats, candles, and a bottle of wine.

Breakfast Strata

You will need to double the recipe for this crowd and use two 9- by 13-inch pans.

1 tablespoon butter or margarine
5 cup (about 1½ to 2 pounds) asparagus
2 cup fresh tomatoes, seeded and cubed
2 cups sliced mushrooms
1 tablespoon fresh chives, chopped
¼ cup fresh chopped basil or 1 tablespoon dried
1 teaspoon grated lemon rind
½ teaspoon salt
1 to 2 good turns with the pepper mill
12 to13 thin slices sandwich bread (about ¼- to ½-inch thick)
cooking spray
1 cup shredded Fontina cheese, divided
2½ cups lowfat milk
4 large eggs
1½ cups breadcrumbs (make your own or use about 1 cup of those already prepared such as Progresso)

Clean asparagus, snap off tough ends about 2 inches from the bottom to remove the tough part of the stem and cut into 1-inch pieces. Place in a plastic bag and microwave for 1 minute. Set aside. (If you are not using a microwave, place in a skillet with about ½ cup water and simmer for about 3 to 4 minutes until crisp but tender.)

Wash tomatoes, cut into 4 sections and remove seeds. Chop into small pieces and set aside. Wash mushrooms and chop into small pieces. Melt butter in small skillet and sauté mushrooms until liquid is evaporated.

In a large bowl, combine the milk, eggs, basil, and chives, lemon rind, and salt and pepper until well blended.

Spray a 13 x 9-inch baking dish with cooking spray and line with half of the bread, piecing together if necessary to cover the entire bottom. Spread half of the asparagus, tomatoes, mushrooms and cheese on the bread. Repeat with the remaining bread, vegetables and cheese.

Gently pour the milk mixture over the strata, cover, and refrigerate overnight or for at least 8 hours.

Preheat oven to 400 degrees. Uncover strata and sprinkle with breadcrumbs. Bake for about 40 minutes until top is brown and a knife, when inserted into the middle, comes out clean. This recipe does not freeze well. It needs to be fresh!

Variation: Substitute artichoke hearts for the asparagus. Use 2 15-ounce cans, drained and chopped. No need to heat.

Fruit Salad

18 cups fresh fruit
¼ cup Grand Marnier liqueur (optional)

Especially in the summer, a simple fruit salad can be wonderful but even in the winter months, it

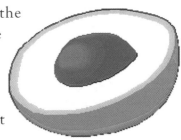

can be quite tasty. Allow about 1 cup of prepared fruit per person but I usually throw in a few extra cups for good measure. (I'm always so worried I won't have enough!)

If you are really pushed for time or energy, you can buy melons that are already cut into bite-sized pieces. Simply add some strawberries, white seedless grapes, and an orange or a peach, or both. This can be made late in the day prior to the event but I don't like to do it earlier than that because it can become soft. If adding bananas, wait until the last minute to cut, mix with about 1 teaspoon of lemon juice, and then add to rest of the fruit right before serving. They can get mushy and turn brown if they set with the rest of the fruit for long periods of time.

If you are starting from scratch, choose melons and other seasonal fruits, wash, and cut into small pieces. I find that a small cantaloupe, when peeled and cut, equals about 4 to 5 cups of fruit; the average apple or peach, when pared and cut, is each about a cup.

Add about ¼ cup of Grand Marnier or your favorite orange liqueur, if desired, to add a bit of zip.

Offer guests small plastic cups or bowls in which they can place the fruit so the juices don't mix with the other foods on their plate.

Mixed Green Salad With Cucumber and Dill Dressing

mixed greens (about 1 handful per person)
1½ cups chopped celery
1½ cups chopped green pepper
1½ cups diced jicama
1 15-ounce can mandarin oranges
3 tablespoons minced fresh mint

You can buy mixed salad greens that only need to be rinsed or choose your favorite lettuces and clean and tear them yourself. Add celery, green peppers, jicama, and mint. Mandarin oranges should be drained and added to the salad right before tossing. Shortly before serving, add the dressing and toss. Start with about ½ cup and add to taste.

Cucumber and Dill Dressing

1 large cucumber
1 tablespoon water
¾ cup vegetable oil
¼ cup red or white wine vinegar
1 teaspoon dried dill or 1 tablespoon fresh chopped dill
¼ teaspoon salt
½ teaspoon sugar

Peel cucumber and cut in half, lengthwise. With a spoon, scoop out and discard seeds. Cut into big chunks. In a blender, combine cucumber, vinegar, and water, and puree until smooth. Add the rest of the ingredients and turn on high until mixed well. Place in dressing container and refrigerate until use. Makes about 2 cups.

Rolls

You can make rolls from scratch (see page 8), or from a box, but I suggest you buy some fresh rolls at the supermarket. If you like, you can place them in a large brown bag, sprinkle with a little water, and place in a hot oven to warm after you have taken the Strata out and turned the oven off. They'll be warm by the time you have put the last-minute touches on the table.

Chocolate Cake and Ice Cream

You can keep this simple too and order a cake from your local bakery or ice cream store. They'll be happy to decorate it according to your theme. But, if you'd rather do it yourself, buy a box cake and follow the directions. If you are having more than 14 to 16 guests, you'll probably need to use 2 cake mixes and bake in 2 9- by 13-inch pans. Be sure to grease the pans generously with butter or oil spray and then dust lightly with flour. Cut a piece of wax paper to fit the bottom of the pans. After the cakes are baked and cooled, gently turn out one cake on to a clean platter and peel off the waxed paper. (A large rectangular cookie sheet, covered with aluminum foil can be used if you don't have a platter large enough for the cake. You can place the cake on a paper lace doily if you wish).

Purchase prepared frosting (found near the cake mixes in the baking section of the grocery store). If making only 1 cake, frost and decorate. You can find tubes of colored icing and small decorations that may be appropriate for your occasion in the same area as the frosting. Party stores will also have lace doilies and items that can be used for cake decorations. If making 2 cakes, turn out the first layer onto the platter with the bottom side facing up, peel off the paper, and frost the top. Gently turn out the second cake, peel off the paper, and put the bottom side down on the top of the frosted layer. Frost the sides and then the top. Decorate.

Store in a cool place until ready to serve. I like to cover with plastic wrap as I normally try to make the cake ahead of time. Place toothpicks in each of the corners and a few in the middle of the cake and lay the wrap over the cake and down the sides. It will probably take two long sheets of wrap, joined in the middle of the cake and place down the sides and secured under the platter.

Purchase your favorite ice cream to serve with the cake.

Iced Tea With Mint Sprigs

1 gallon water
3 tea bags
Lemon wedges
Sugar
artificial sweeteners
fresh mint, washed and cut into small sprigs

Put water in a large pan and place on stove to heat. As soon as steam starts to rise, turn off the heat and put in 3 of your favorite tea bags. Let steep for about 45 minutes to 1 hour. Remove bags and place in container or pitcher in the refrigerator to cool. Serve over ice with lemon wedges and mint and an assortment of sugar and artificial sweeteners.

Timetable

This is perhaps one of the easiest menus to get on the table on time because so much can be done the day before the event.

1 day before the event:
· If table is inside, decorate and set it; don't forget tea, juice, wine glasses, and coffee cups.
· Cut celery, jicama and pepper for salad.
· Wash and tear lettuce and mix with celery and pepper; place in plastic bags and refrigerate.
· Make salad dressing and refrigerate.
· Make rolls and bake. When room temperature, store in plastic bags.
· Make cake and decorate.
· Make strata but do not bake; cover with plastic wrap and refrigerate.
· Pour orange juice into pitcher(s), cover with plastic wrap, and refrigerate.
· Late in the day, make the fruit salad (except for banana).
· Place nuts in serving dishes and cover with plastic wrap.
· Make tea and refrigerate.
· Cut lemon in wedges for tea, cover, and refrigerate.
· Wash mint. Cut some into sprigs for tea and chop 3 tablespoons for the green salad.

1 hour and 15 minutes
    before (guests begin to arrive):
· If you have been at an event and return home at the same time your guests arrive, ask a family member or one of your guests to assist you in opening wine or champagne.
· Preheat oven to 400 degrees.
· Make first pot of coffee and turn on.
· Set out mixed nuts.
· Place sugar, cream, artificial sweetener, lemon wedges, and ice on table.
· Place iced tea, orange juice on table with champagne and wine; ask guests to help themselves.
· As soon as coffee is made, pour into carafe, and place on the table. Make a second pot immediately.

1 hour before:
· Put Strata in oven.
· Finish Fruit Salad and return to refrigerator.
· Add mandarin oranges to green salad and toss but don't add dressing just yet.
· Make another pot of coffee; if not needed yet at least fix the grounds so they are ready.

20 minutes before:
· Take strata out of oven and turn oven off.
· Place rolls in a brown paper bag and sprinkle with a little water; place in oven to warm.
· Place butter on table.

- Ask someone to open additional wine and Champagne and place on table.
- Refresh the tea, orange juice, and put out a pitcher of milk on table for children.

10 minutes before:
- Cut Strata into servings and place on table. Cover with foil.
- Toss salad with dressing and place on table.
- Place Fruit Salad on table.

5 minutes before:
- Take rolls out of oven and place in basket.
- Check coffee and make another pot if necessary.

Brunch time:
- Remove foil from strata and call guests to the table. Take a moment to toast the honored guest and enjoy!

Dessert time:
- Clear dishes; pour another cup of coffee or wine.
- Cut cake and serve with ice cream. Enjoy! Cleanup will be easy especially if you've used paper and plastic utensils.

Tip: Need just a little butter in a skillet to saute a few onions or an egg? Take a whole stick of butter, unwrap one end, and just rub it around the surface of a hot skillet. You can get just what you need to coat the bottom without having to use a spoon or knife. Just close up the wrapper and put it back into the refrigerator.

Shopping List

Check your pantry for these staples. Add those you are missing to your weekly shopping list.

- ____salt
- ____pepper
- ____cooking spray
- ____red or white wine vinegar
- ____vegetable oil
- ____dried dill
- ____sugar
- ____flour
- ____waxed paper
- ____plastic wrap
- ____tea
- ____artificial sweeteners
- ____ice
- ____coffee

Don't forget to calculate how much you will need to have each item based on the number of guests you expect. Here's what you'll need to add to your weekly shopping list:

- ____margarine (strata, rolls, cake pans)
- ____Fontina cheese (strata)
- ____vanilla ice cream (dessert)
- ____lowfat milk (strata and drinking)
- ____eggs (strata)
- ____mandarin oranges, canned (green salad)
- ____breadcrumbs (strata)
- ____roll mix or rolls
- ____cake mix (dessert)
- ____frosting (dessert)
- ____decorating items (dessert)
- ____bread slices, ¼- to ½-inch thick (strata)
- ____cucumbers (salad dressing)
- ____mixed nuts (appetizer)
- ____celery (green salad)
- ____jicama (green salad)
- ____green pepper (green salad)
- ____asparagus (strata)
- ____tomatoes (strata)
- ____salad greens
- ____mushrooms (strata)
- ____fresh chives (strata)
- ____fresh basil (strata)
- ____fresh mint (green salad and tea)
- ____fresh dill (salad dressing)
- ____lemon (strata, iced tea)
- ____seasonal fruit such as strawberries, melons, banana, peaches, and so forth(fruit salad)
- ____orange juice
- ____wine or champagne
- ____Grand Marnier
- ____doily (cake)
- ____ice

Shopping List Amounts

To serve:	8	16	24
margarine	1 cup + 1 tablespoon	2 cups + 2 tablespoons	3cups+3tablespoons
fontina cheese	1 cup	2 cup	3 cup
vanilla ice cream	1/2 gallon	1 gallon	1 gallon
low fat milk	2 1/2 cups + drinking	5 cups + drinking	7 1/2 cups + drinking
eggs	4	8	12
mandarin oranges	7-ounce can	15-ounce can	7- + 15-ounce cans
breadcrumbs	1 1/2 cups	3 cups	4 1/2 cups
roll mix or rolls	1 box (1 dozen)	2 boxes (2 dozen)	3 boxes (21/2 dozen)
cake mix	1	1	2
frosting	1 to 2 cans	1 to 2 cans	2 to 4 cans
additional frosting colors	as desired	as desired	as desired
cake decorating items	as desired	as desired	as desired
bread ¼ to ½ inch thick	12 to 13 slices	24 to 26 slices	36 to 39 slices
cucumbers	1	1	1
mixed nuts	1 lb	2 lbs	3 lbs
celery	3/4 cup	1 1/2 cups	1 3/4 cups
jicama	1/2 small	1 small	1 large
asparagus	1 1/2 to 2 lbs	3 to 4 lbs	5 to 6 lbs
tomatoes	2 medium	4 medium	6 medium
salad greens	8 cups (1 1/2 lbs)	16 cups (3 lbs)	24 cups (4 lbs)
mushrooms	10 medium	20 medium	30 medium
fresh chives	1 small bunch	1 small bunch	1 small bunch
fresh basil	1 small bunch	1 small bunch	1 small bunch
fresh mint	1 small bunch	1 small bunch	1 small bunch
fresh dill	1 small bunch	1 small bunch	1 small bunch
lemon	2	3	4
seasonal fruit: cantalope, peach, banana, strawberries	1 cantalope, 1 peach, 1 banana, 1 pint strawberries	double	triple
orange juice	1 gallon	2 gallons	3 gallons
wine/ champagne	will depend on number of wine, champagne, and mimosa drinkers; if only mimosa drinkers, 6 to 8 drinks per bottle of champagne; for wine drinkers, figure 1/3 to ½ bottle per person		
doily			
ice			
camera			

Ordering Information

Yes, I want to order_____copies of *DinnerOnTime: Holiday & Special Occasion Cooking Preparation Guidelines & Shopping Lists* at $21.95 each plus $4 shipping. (Colorado residents add 3% sales tax per book.) Please allow 3 weeks for delivery.

Name _____

Address _____

City/state/zip _____

Telephone _____

Email _____

My check is enclosed for $ _____

Please charge my Visa or Mastercard

Account number _____exp_____

Signature _____

Make your check payable and return to:

DinnerOnTime

PO Box 261283, Highlands Ranch, CO 80163

Credit card orders can be phoned to 303/346-0219

Order on the Web at: www.DinnerOnTime.com